HIT AND RUN LESSONS:

Mastering the Trading Strategies

∎∎

Jeff Cooper

M. GORDON PUBLISHING GROUP

Los Angeles, California

ISBN 1-893756-05-X

Printed in the United States of America

Disclaimer

Past results are not indicative of future returns. The publisher, the author, and their affiliates make no claim to the future effectiveness of the methods described in this book. Examples in this book are for educational purposes only. This is not a solicitation of any order to buy or sell. There is a high degree of risk in trading.

CONTENTS

ACKNOWLEDGMENTS

▫ ▫

I would like to give special thanks to David Landry, Danilo Torres, Judy Brown, and Eddie Kwong for the help they provided me in creating this book.

INTRODUCTION

••

Four years ago, I first started writing about the strategies I use to make a living trading stocks short-term. Many of these strategies were published in my two books, *Hit and Run Trading I* and *II.*

Since then, I have continued to earn profits, year after year, using exactly the same strategies that I wrote about in these books. Even more gratifying is that I have witnessed many other success stories besides my own.

There is nothing magical about my success or any of these other people: Everyday I work hard and for longer hours than most people work in their conventional jobs. But the payoff is freedom, a big check, and the skills I need to earn that paycheck for an entire lifetime.

In coming up with this book, I asked myself:

What is it that separates those who experience consistent success with trading, versus those who do not?

In my opinion it is:

The thought process that occurs between recognizing a trading setup, analyzing it, and then doing something constructive about it.

This book, *Hit and Run Lessons*, contains that very thought process. The way in which I'm going to share this with you is by showing you something that very few people get to see.

Over the past four years, I have run a trading service limited to a small number of traders. In it, I talk about the trading setups I'm watching and trading from day to day. One of the most important features is what I call my *Daily Learning Sheets*. In these, I explain exactly what is going through my mind when I look at different real-time trading setups and apply the same strategies that I've been teaching in my books. As I look back at what is contained in these Daily Learning Sheets, I notice that there are many valuable observations I make about the way in which my strategies appear in real market conditions. These observations are, I believe, a key ingredient to my success.

The following sections contain the very best of my Daily Learning Sheets, exactly as they originated from my head. With the exception of glaring grammatical and spelling errors, they are all presented as they were originally. That's the only way to give you a true insider's peak at my observations and insights.

The first and largest section deals with my favorite strategy, Stepping In Front Of Size (SIFOS). If I could only trade one strategy, this would be it. I have made consistent profits from SIFOS over the years and I will show you the many twists and turns you can use to apply it to your own trading.

Section 2 covers pullbacks. I, along with many other traders, have profited from the fact that strongly trending markets pullback before resuming their trend. I will show you how to identify the best pullbacks and when to enter them.

Section 3 looks at trading multiple signals. As I have stated in the past, when two, three, or four setups are simultaneously pointing in the same direction, it increases your chances of the trade being a success.

In Section 4, I will teach you a handful of strategies and patterns that you can add to your daily trading repertoire.

In Section 5, the final section, we will look at when and how to lock in profits. Money management is an essential piece of my methodology (and all good trading methodologies) and I believe this section will do more to improve your trading than any other section in the book.

Before proceeding, let me point a few things out ahead of time:

1. All of these sheets were selected for their educational value. Their order varies by section.

2. Some of these trades never triggered. As you know, for a buy setup to trigger, the stock must trade 1/16 above the previous day's high; for a sell-short signal, the stock has to trade 1/16 below the previous day's low.

3. A few of the charts were never scanned and are therefore a bit faded. My decision was to include them because of their educational value to you.

4. With the exception of glaring errors, I have reprinted the original text. This is the best way I know of you getting into my mind as things happened that day.

5. Final note—Re-read my first two books. Then read, re-read, and read again these examples. Also, if you can, download the charts on your computer and look at them within the context of the bigger picture market happenings at that time. The more effort you put into this, the more knowledge you will have and the more success you will achieve.

Now, let's move onto Section One.

Section I

STEPPING IN FRONT OF SIZE

∎ ∎

If you've read my first two Hit and Run books, you've heard me say that I consider Stepping In Front Of Size to be one of my bread-and-butter strategies. That's still true today. When you think about it, it makes sense. There is no other strategy that I know of that allows you to probe so deeply into the minds of size traders such as institutions.

I like to think of it as a game of high-stakes poker in which one of the rules says that I get walk behind each opponent and study their hands and place my bets with whomever's got the winning hand.

Because institutions are forced to buy and sell in large blocks of shares it's hard for them to avoid belly flopping in or out of a stock when they put up bids or offers in small-cap stocks. That creates a big splash that I can see through my Time and Sales data. Not only are their true intentions revealed, but also I figure they've got to know that something's going to happen in the stock or else they wouldn't be messing with these no-name stocks. If they're really desperate, as is frequently the case when their order is placed in the last hour of trading, I know they've got to own or dump the stock no matter what. That will push the stock either up and down. Many times it is no different than you sailing with a solid breeze to your back.

One final note. In further confirmation to the validity of this strategy, I was speaking recently at a live forum on TRADEHARD.COM with

Kevin Haggerty, who used to run Fidelity Capital Markets' trading desk. In front of thousands of traders he said to me, "Guys like you and strategies like this are what made my job so difficult." To me this was the highest complement I could be paid.

I have laid out this section in the following order. Size to Buy at New Highs (my favorite strategy) is covered on pages 7 to 14. Stepping In Front Of Substantial Size (10,000 or more shares on the bid) goes from pages 15 to 20. Size to Buy combined with Multiple Setups is shown on pages 21 to 29. Offering Knockouts (buyers taking out large sellers in strongly uptrending stocks) is looked at on pages 30 to 35. And finally, on pages 36 to 44 I added some additional Stepping In Front Of Size examples for you to look at.

COOPER TRADING INC.
DAILY LEARNING SHEET
Monday, 12 October 1998

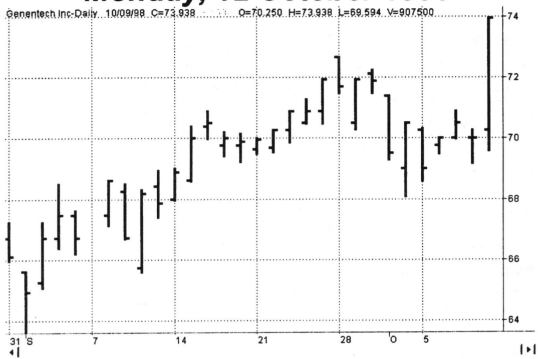

Genentech Inc-Daily 10/09/98 C=73.938   O=70.250 H=73.938 L=69.594 V=907500

Reading Size: Size To Buy Taking Out The Morning Range, Size Offer Knockouts At/Near Recent Highs

Because GNE (a stock on the Small Cap Hit List) has held up well during the current market turbulence, the stock was a good candidate to stalk for size buyers: If they're not going down in the squall, there's a good likelihood that they're going up when the market lifts. That's what occurred with GNE Friday. After a morning pullback, a <u>substantial size buyer</u> (10,000 shares at 70 1/8 at 12:56pm) <u>appears near the early session highs</u> suggesting the stock would make further highs on the day. At 1:01pm 5000 shares is bid the uptick at 70 5/8. At 1:34pm, a very substantial size bid for 25,000 shares at 71 appears. Then at 1:38pm, another large bid for 10000 shares steps up to 71 1/8. At 3:29pm <u>a size offer of 15,000 shares near prior recent highs</u> is knocked out.

In this example, the tale of the tape teaches us to look for a few things:
1) Size to buy at/near the morning range high (particularly after an early pullback) is often a good indication that the stock has further to run.
2) Size offers knocked out and/or size bids near prior daily highs is often a tip-off to a breakout.

Size bids often indicate an "agenda": once an institution makes a decision to buy (or) sell that impetus doesn't fade quickly. Even if the stock doesn't explode immediately, as long as the stock holds firm, the buyer usually is lurking in the wings; if no stock comes his way, they must step up their attack. Reading size on the tape will help increase your success.

COOPER TRADING INC.
DAILY LEARNING SHEET
Friday, 9 April 1999

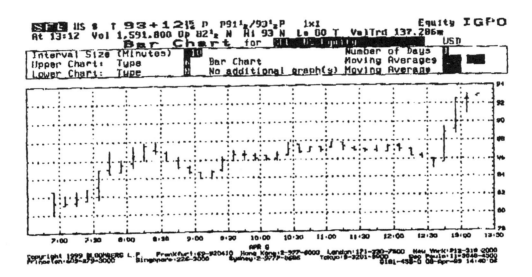

Size Offer KO's at new Highs

When all systems are go and the market is in gear, momentum names can rocket to unimagined levels. That is where the action is. That's where to concentrate. SFE has been on the small cap list for a few weeks. In spite of the fact that the volume on the stock has mushroomed since the expansion breakout on 3/11 (coming off a weekly cup and handle with a long base), the stock still behaves like a small cap stock; it responds to size bids and offers and as you can see, since it is a thin issue, the stock really explodes when buyers overwhelm sellers.

SFE consolidated early morning gains by trading sideways most of the afternoon. However, between 12:15pm (PST) and 12:30pm (PST) there was a quick flush out which tested the resolve of short-term traders, most likely stopping many out.

However, the test of a superior trader is the ability to re-enter on a continuation move. When SFE probes close to a test of the 9am to 9:30am (PST) lows, leaving a tail, it is time to stalk the stock. Here is what happened;

At 12:45pm PST (15 minutes before the close) a size offer of 6,100 shares at 88 is knocked out. Then, at 12:50pm (PST), a size offer of 13,700 shares at 90 is lifted immediately. SFE goes out at 93, 5 points higher than where the late day buying interest appeared 15 minutes before the bell.

Conclusion: Momentum stocks during strong trend days tend to close at/near the high of the day. When this occurs with 1) the market in gear, 2) with the stock at new highs, and 3) large buying interest late in the session, these momentum explosions can create big profits very quickly.

COOPER TRADING INC.
DAILY LEARNING SHEET
17 NOVEMBER 1997

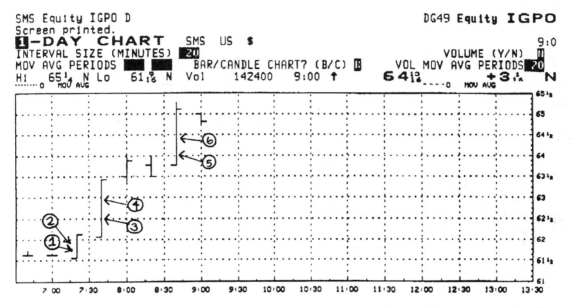

SMS Equity IGPO D
Screen printed.
1-DAY CHART   SMS US $ 9:0
INTERVAL SIZE (MINUTES) **20**   VOLUME (Y/N) **N**
MOV AVG PERIODS **■** **■**   BAR/CANDLE CHART? (B/C) **B**   VOL MOV AVG PERIODS **20**
Hi 65¼ N Lo 61⅞ N Vol   142400   9:00 ↑   **64½**----○   **+3¼**   N

DG49 Equity **IGPO**

Stepping In Front Of Size at New Highs

Yesterday's set-up sheet showed that SMS was at a new 60 day high. This fact should alert you to look at the chart where it becomes apparent that the stock has been very stable and virtually unaffected by this week's wild intraday market gyrations. In other words, SMS held onto recent gains easily. Yesterday's sheet also reflected a *CTI* of 2-3, a <u>still</u> oversold market in spite of an 86 point rally. Consequently, if the market was going to rally on Friday, there would be a strong likelihood for SMS to lead.

Putting the above pieces together told us to focus on SMS Friday morning: to stalk the stock. Here's what transpired:

    ① 7:15 PST 10,000 shares (size) is bid at 61 5/8.
    ② 7:18   The bid is raised slightly to 61 11/16 and we buy at the market.

    ③ 7:36 PST A 9,000 share buyer appears at 62 1/2.
    ④ 7:40   A 10,000 share bid shows up at 63 as the stock explodes.

    ⑤ 8:38 PST 18,000 shares is bid at 64.
    ⑥ 8:39   The bid (10,00 shs.) is raised to 64 1/4 and the stock leaps again.

Using our Stepping In Front Of Size strategy combined with new highs is a terrific way to maximize the profit potential of the *Small Cap Hit List.*

COOPER TRADING INC.
DAILY LEARNING SHEET
Monday, 19 October 1998

Perkin Elmer Corp-Daily 10/16/98 C=76.000 · · · O=73.750 H=77.375 L=73.375

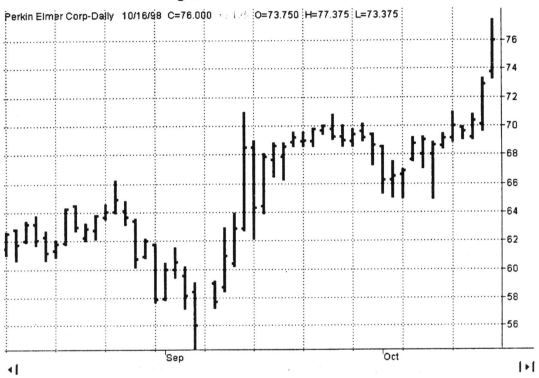

Stepping In Front Of Size At New Highs

PKN has been bucking the overall market turbulence since late August. On the fax dated 10/14, I showed the Extension Level Boomer set-up on PKN and noted the new closing high. Often a new closing high anticipates a breakout. This is what occurred with PKN on Thursday giving us a solid gain. The Flat Top Breakout continued today; the tip off – Stepping In Front Of Size (SIFOS) at new highs – substantial size to buy (10,000 at 75) created a further 2 point profit.

Size at new highs is a good indication that momentum spurts will continue.

Cooper Trading Inc.
DAILY LEARNING SHEET
1 October 1997

```
                    M A R K E T / T R A D E   R E C A P              Page 9
     Time  ██:██   Min Vol ██x100      Volumes scaled by 100
     Date  █9/3█  Price Range ██████  To ██████
LONE STAR TECHNOLOGIES 1 (LSS    US)              PRICE 52³₁₆    N     $
 Time   E   Bid/Trd/Ask    E    Size    Cond  Time  E   Bid/Trd/Ask   E    Size    Cond
10:02 M    ↓50⁷₈                5           09:45 N     51/51¹₈      B    10x1
09:58 N   50⁷₈/51³₁₆    N    5x5           09:45 N     51/51⁵₁₆     T    10x5     TRIM
09:58 T   50⁷₈/51³₁₆    N    5x5    TRIM   09:45 N    50⁷₈/51⁵₁₆    T    5x5      TRIM
09:58 N    ↓51               4           09:45 N     51³₁₆              8
09:58 N   51/51¹₁₆    N    2x5           09:45 N    ↑51³₁₆             5
09:58 N   51/51¹₂     N    2x5           09:44 M     51               10
09:58 N    51¹₁₆              3           09:44 N   50⁷₈/51¹₄    N    5x5
09:58 N   ↓51¹₁₆             2           09:44 N   50⁷₈/51¹₈    X    5x1
09:54 N   51¹₁₆/51¹₂    N    5x5           09:44 N   50⁷₈/51¹₁₆    T    5x5      TRIM
09:54 B   51¹₈/51¹₂    N    1x5           09:44 N   50³₄/51¹₁₆    T    5x5      TRIM
09:54 T   51³₁₆/51³₈    N    5x5    TRIM   09:44 N     51                50   ②
09:54 X   51¹₄/51¹₂    N    1x5           09:44 N     51                22
09:53 N    51³₁₆              5           09:44 N   50³₄/51      N    5x72
09:53 N   51⁵₁₆/51³₂    N    5x5           09:44 N     51                41   ②
09:51 N   51¹₁₆/51¹₄    N    5x5           09:36 M     51               10
09:51 N   51/51¹₂     N    10x5           09:36 N   50³₄/51      N    5x115 ①
09:51 N   ↑51⁷₁₆             8           09:35 N     51               10
09:45 N   51/51⁷₁₆    N    10x5           09:34 T    ↓51               11
     Bloomberg·all rights reserved    Frankfurt·69.920410   Hong Kong·2.521.3000   London·171.330.7500   New York·212.318.2000
```

Taking Out A Large Offer On A New High

As many of you know, Stepping in Front of Size on new highs is a valuable and profitable strategy. Another angle to this theme is to look for large blocks of stock for sale on a thinly traded stock that is trading at new highs. If this block is eliminated by buyers, you know the momentum players are focused on this stock and are taking it higher.

Today, LSS had a large seller ① at 51 as the stock made all time highs. As you can see ② the seller was quickly taken out and this indicated that more buying than selling was prevalent. The stock proceeded to close at 52 3/16 on an Expansion Breakout.

Look for this type of situation whenever you can as it many times lead to further price appreciation.

COOPER TRADING INC.
DAILY LEARNING SHEET
Monday, 02 November 1998

Sofamor/Danek Group I-Daily   10/30/98 C=101.625 +4.437 O=97.188 H=102.000 L=97.188 V=252600

REPRINTED WITH PERMISSION OF OMEGA RESEARCH INC.
Chart created using Omega SuperCharts 4.0.

Monitoring the Hit List and Anticipating Large Range Breakouts with Stepping In Front Of Size

One of the best ways to anticipate a large range breakout is the appearance of size bids at/near new highs. SDG (on our Hit List) is a good example of when to monitor a stock for Stepping In Front of Size. Both Wednesday and Thursday, the stock closed at new all time highs. In and of itself, this is a clue to focus on the stock. Then early in Friday's session (9:47am EST) 20,000 shares trades at 98, the old high. As you know volume typically precedes price, and that's just what happened. At 9:53am EST, a 5000 share bid appears at 98. Immediately thereafter (9:54am EST), a 5000 share bidder leapfrogs our first friend, stepping up to 98 3/4. There is an obvious urgency to own the stock as another bid for 5000 shares shows up at 99 (9:56am EST). SDG trades up to 100 3/4 before "flat lining" but closes on its high at 101 5/8. When there is size to buy and the stock won't come in, allowing the buyers to fill, it is usually a good bet that the stock will move higher in the final hour as the frustrated buyer(s) are forced to pay up. Keep this in mind as it offers you an opportunity to capture further profits. Remember the old adage: stocks in a strong trend day tend to close at/near their high.

COOPER TRADING INC.
DAILY LEARNING SHEET
Monday, 21 December 1998

Bre-X Minerals Ltd-Daily 12/18/98 C=55.625 +4.062 O=51.438 H=55.875 L=51.125

REPRINTED WITH PERMISSION OF OMEGA RESEARCH INC.
Chart created using Omega SuperCharts 4.0.

Size To Buy At/Near New 60 Day Highs

On last night's set-up sheet, I showed the Expansion Breakout on BXM, Size bids (6100 at 51 3/4, 10:19am EST and 5000 at 51 15/16, 12:22pm EST) were clues that the set-up would trigger. When substantial size (10,000 shares) to buy at new highs showed up at 53 (2:14pm EST), the stock exploded to 55 7/8. When size shows up in the last few hours, it usually means the players are stepping up to bat because nothing is coming in. It is a good idea to treat size to buy with a single signal as a multiple set-up.

COOPER TRADING INC.
LEARNING SHEET
Monday, 21 June 1999

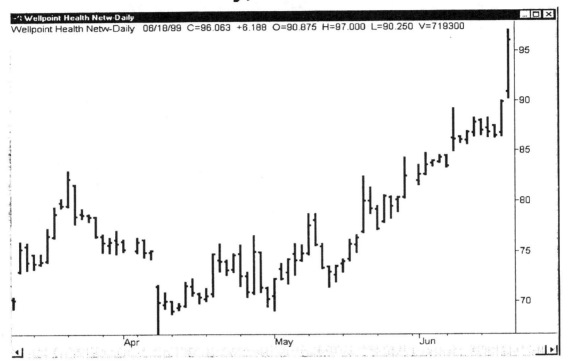

Wellpoint Health Netw-Daily
Wellpoint Health Netw-Daily 06/18/99 C=96.063 +6.188 O=90.875 H=97.000 L=90.250 V=719300

PRINTED WITH PERMISSION OF OMEGA RESEARCH INC.
Charts created using Omega Super Charts 4.0

OFFERS AT NEW HIGHS

Although WLP opened on a gap of 7/8 of a point overriding our trigger by 1/8 of a point, stalking the stock would have provided an opportunity to capture solid profits.

After trading in a narrow range the majority of the session, a size offer of 10,000 at 91 9/16 is knocked out at 2:06 (ET) just below session highs, another size offer of 5,000 shares at 92 is lifted at 2:16 and WLP goes bid the uptick with 5,000 bid for at 92.

Throughout the last hour this pattern of size offers taken and size bids on an uptick suggested WLP could get dragged into the bell as today was expiration. When WLP crossed 95 it immediately exploded to 97—such is the power of size offers knocked out and size bids at new highs—particularly on expiration Friday.

COOPER TRADING INC.
DAILY LEARNING SHEET
FRIDAY, 28 AUGUST 1998

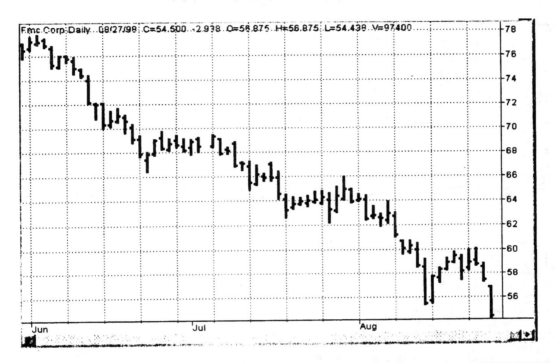

Fmc Corp Daily 08/27/98 C=54.500 -2.938 O=56.875 H=56.875 L=54.438 V=97,400

Stepping In Front Of Substantial Size For Sale

Getting off a short sale when a size seller shows his hand is a tougher strategy to execute than taking the offer when a size buyer appears due to the need for an uptick. However, you do get filled more often than you think and you should definitely look to capitalize on this strategy, as stocks can fall rapidly when forced selling (mutual fund redemptions, margin calls) sets in.

Today, FMC, on our Small Cap downtrend list, had a size seller of 20,000 shares at 57 just after the open. After trading at 56 11/16, FMC upticked at 56 13/16. The seller persisted and the next uptick didn't occur until 55 1/2. However, FMC closed on its low at 54 1/2 creating a solid gain. When you see substantial size for sale in a small cap stock in a strong downtrend, it is often an indication of a decision by a fund manager(s) to unload a stock. Keep an eye out for size offers on stocks at/near new lows as this often leads to an Expansion Breakdown day.

COOPER TRADING INC.
DAILY LEARNING SHEET
Thursday, 01 October 1998

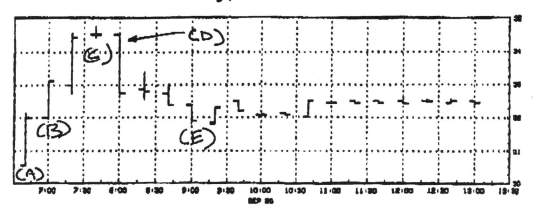

Entering, Adding, Trailing and Exiting

By combining Stepping In Front Of Size (SIFOS) strategies with Small Cap set-ups you will improve your overall trading. KUH, shown as a low-level Expansion Pivot on Wednesday's fax, provided a great example today. At 0932 (EST) there was a size bid of 5,000 shares at 30 1/2 (A). This should alert you that the set-up is worth trading. At 0934 the bid is raised to 30 3/4. In combination with the Expansion Pivot, we now have a Stepping In Front Of Size buy. At 0937 the bid is raised to 31 1/8. With size behind you, this is a good time to add to your position. At 1001 a block of 10,000 shares is bid for at 32 1/16 (B). This substantial size suggests that someone is very eager to buy the shares. At this juncture, aggressive traders may want to continue to add to their position by Stepping In Front Of Substantial Size. At 1004 the bid is raised to 32 1/4. This confirms that the buyer is very eager. The stock quickly trades up to 34 1/2, a gain of over 4 points from the prior day's close. At 1058 a large block of 26,000 is sold at 34 1/4 (C). This suggests that the buyer may be satisfied. It is a good time to sell a piece of your position and tighten your stop on the remainder. At 1100 a substantial size offer of 20,000 shares is offered at 34 3/8 (D). This is further evidence that the buying has dried up and the sellers have returned. It is a good time to continue taking profits. Shortly thereafter, the stock implodes and within the next hour trades over 2 points lower than its high(E). As you can see, SIFOS and time and sale screens are valuable when it comes to entering positions, adding to positions, trailing stops and exiting positions.

GAP RULE: Any buy recommendation that opens 3/4 point above the stated entry price and any sell recommendation that opens 3/4 point below the stated entry price should be ignored for the day.

Reminder...A signal is not valid unless it trades at or above the entry price for buys and at or below the entry price for short sales

Charts created using SuperCharts® by Omega Research, Inc.   Copyright @ 1998, Cooper Trading, Inc.

COOPER TRADING, INC.
DAILY LEARNING SHEET
04 NOVEMBER 1997

Revlon Inc.-CL A (REV)

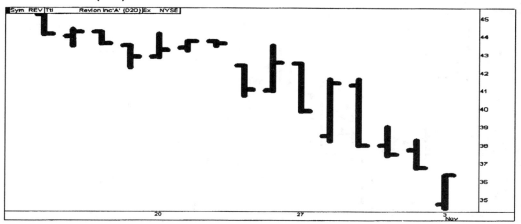

Time	E	Bid/Trd/Ask	E	Size	Time	E	Bid/Trd/Ask	E	Size
13:03	M	$36^1{}_8/36^3{}_8$	P	1x1	12:51	N	$36^1{}_8/36^1{}_4$	X	171X1
13:02	N	$\uparrow36^3{}_8$	M	15	12:51	N	$36^1{}_4$		20
12:59	N	$36^1{}_4/36^3{}_8$	M	207X20	12:50	N		N	191X3
12:59	N	$36^1{}_4/36^3{}_8$		207X10	12:48	N	$36^1{}_8/36^5{}_{16}$	N	119X5
12:59	N	$36^1{}_4$	X	8	12:47	N	$36^1{}_8/36^3{}_8$		191X10
12:59	N	$\downarrow36^1{}_4$	M	1	12:47	N	$\uparrow36^1{}_4$	N	6
12:59	N	$36^1{}_4/36^3{}_8$		216X10	12:46	N	$\downarrow36^3{}_{16}$	N	2
12:59	N	$36^1{}_4/36^3{}_8$		1X10	12:46	N	$36^1{}_8/36^3{}_8$	N	186X10
12:59	N	$\uparrow36^3{}_8$	N	1	12:46	N	$36^1{}_8/36^1{}_4$	N	186X1
12:56	C	$36^1{}_4/36^3{}_8$	N	215X10	12:45	N	$36^1{}_8/36^1{}_4$		20X5
12:56	N	$\downarrow36^1{}_4$	N	8	12:45	N	$36^1{}_4$	N	4
12:55	N	$36^1{}_4/36^3{}_8$		216X2	12:44	M	$36^1{}_4$		5
12:54	N	$36^1{}_4/36^3{}_8$		166X2	12:43	N	$\uparrow36^1{}_4$		3
12:54	N	$\uparrow36^3{}_8$	N	2	12:42	N	$36^1{}_8/36^1{}_4$	N	20X10
12:53	N	$36^1{}_4/36^1{}_2$	N	166X20	12:42	N	$36^1{}_8/36^1{}_4$	N	20X1
12:53	N	$36^1{}_4/36^3{}_8$		166X1	12:42	C	$\downarrow36$		4
12:53	N	$36^1{}_4/36^3{}_8$		166X10	12:42	N	$\uparrow36^1{}_8$	N	25
12:52	**N**	$\mathbf{36^1{}_8/36^3{}_8}$	**N**	**171X10**	12:42		$/36^1{}_8$		X19

We have a Gilligan buy set-up for Tuesday on REV (Revlon). The stock has been on a sharp downtrending spiral since trading above 53 only 8 weeks ago. Today, the stock gapped lower and reversed sharply closing on its high for the day. Also, please note the size of the buyer who was bidding for the stock late in the day. On average, REV only trades 60k-80k shares per day and a buyer of this size can certainly push prices higher before he/she gets completely filled.

COOPER TRADING INC.
DAILY LEARNING SHEET
Friday, 18 September 1998

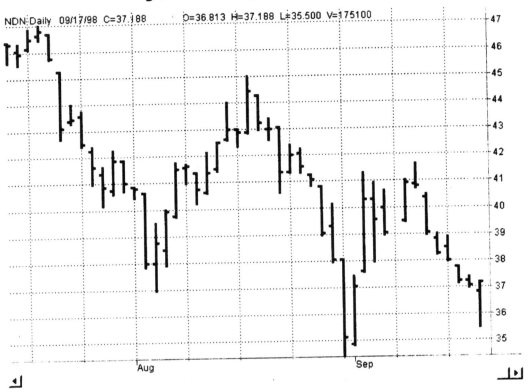

NDN Daily 09/17/98 C=37.188   O=36.813 H=37.188 L=35.500 V=175100

Lizard Test

Here's a short and sweet analysis of a set-up for Friday. NDN is a Lizard buy with the benefit of 2 other positive pieces.

1) The Lizard occurred in the area of the August 31st – September 1st reversal. In other words, buyers appeared near prior support, creating what appears to be a successful test of the lows (at least short-term).

2) Also, there was a <u>substantial</u> size buyer of 20,000 shares on the close. This is a very large bid for a stock this thin and suggests follow through for Friday.

Whenever you have a signal and there is size to buy (or sell in the case of a short set-up) it's a good idea to treat it as a multiple signal.

COOPER TRADING INC. DAILY LEARNING SHEET
11 MAY 1998

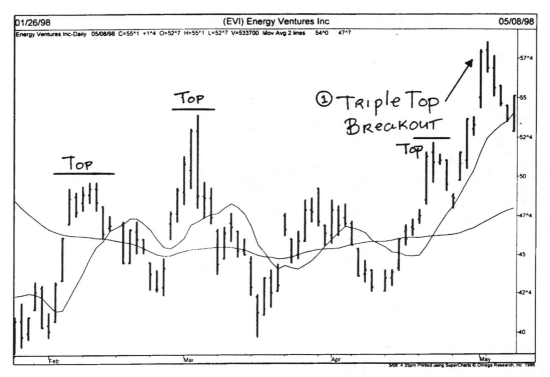

Reprinted with permission of Omega Research Inc.
Chart created using Omega SuperCharts 4.0.

Not All 180s Are Created Equal

Obviously, not all 180s are going to occur at a similar position of strength (or weakness) in a stock. Tonight, we have an example of a 180 that is interesting for a few reasons. The week before last, I mentioned in the "Gleamings" that in my opinion, demand in the oil service sector was back in control.

Here we have EVI, a familiar name to long-term subscribers, and a leading stock in the oil service group. Friday's action in EVI leaves us with an outside day (lower low, higher high) 180. Coming on the heels of the first pullback after a breakout over triple tops ① creates a good likelihood for follow through Monday. Furthermore, a underline substantial offer of 20,000 shares was swallowed in the last hour of trading Friday, reflecting a large appetite on the part of a buyer(s). Let's stalk EVI for a sign of this buyer reappearing Monday.

Looking for these snap backs (in the direction of the trend) with outside days, with wider range days, and/or after 1st pullbacks will add to your success.

COOPER TRADING INC.
DAILY LEARNING SHEET
8 OCTOBER 1997

VTS Equity QRM
Screen printed.

DG49 **Equity Q R M**

M A R K E T / T R A D E   R E C A P
Volumes scaled by 100

Page 1

Time ___:__　Min Vol **100**
Date **10/ 7**　Price Range ▓▓▓▓▓ To ▓▓▓▓▓

VERITAS DGC INC　　　　(VTS　US)　　　PRICE 46⁷₈　　N　　$

Time	E	Bid/Trd/Ask	E	Size	Cond	Time	E	Bid/Trd/Ask	E	Size	Cond
13:18	P	46⁵₈/47	P	6x1		12:47	N	↓46³₄		2	
13:05	P	46⁵₈/47	X	6x1		12:46	N	46¹¹₁₆		49	
13:03	M	46³₄/47	X	10x1		12:45	N	46¹¹₁₆		2	
13:01	N	↑46⁷₈		43		12:45	N	46¹¹₁₆		2	
13:00	M	46³₄/47	B	10x1		12:44	N	46³₄/46¹¹₁₆	N	253x100	
13:00	M	46³₄/46¹⁵₁₆	P	10x1		12:39	N	46¹¹₁₆		2	
13:00	M	46³₄/46¹⁵₁₆	T	10x5	TRIM	12:39	N	↑46¹¹₁₆		2	
13:00	M	46³₄/46⁷₈	X	10x1		12:38	N	46³₄/46¹¹₁₆	N	250x100	
12:58	N	46¹¹₁₆		1		12:34	N	46³₄/46¹¹₁₆	N	250x150	
12:57	M	46¹¹₁₆		1		12:34	N	46³₄/46¹¹₁₆	N	250x128	
12:52	N	46³₄/46¹¹₁₆	N	100x23		12:34	B	↓46³₄		10	
12:51	N	46³₄/46¹³₁₆	N	100x13		12:33	N	46¹¹₁₆		10	
12:51	N	46¹¹₁₆		6		12:33	N	46¹¹₁₆		10	
12:51	N	46³₄/46¹³₁₆	N	100x19		12:32	N	46¹¹₁₆		15	
12:50	N	46³₄/46¹¹₁₆	N	253x19		12:32	N	46³₄/46¹¹₁₆	N	250x100	
12:50	N	46¹¹₁₆		152		12:32	N	↑46¹¹₁₆		15	
12:49	N	46¹¹₁₆		4		12:32	N	46³₄/46¹¹₁₆	N	100x100	
12:49	M	↑46¹¹₁₆		4		12:31	N	46³₄		224	

Veritas (VTS) has a 180 set-up on Wednesday but what makes it even more intriguing is the size of the buyer near the close. Whenever a small cap stock has a buyer of this magnitude, it is a fairly low risk trade to step in front of him and then place your protective stop 1/8 under his bid.

Watch for this buyer in the morning to see if he shows up again.

COOPER TRADING INC.
DAILY LEARNING SHEET
Thursday, 24 September 1998

Waters Corp-Daily 09/23/98 C=65.625 · O=62.750 H=66.000 L=62.750 V=241200

Multiple Set-Up With Substantial Size to Buy

WAT is a name on our Small Cap up trending Hit List. Always remember to monitor these names for size buyers when the market is in rally mode, (as it was on Wednesday). A lot of time goes into choosing the best relative strength names for the list. When the market is in gear and there is size to buy on a strong stock, you have the benefit of three positive pieces working for you. For example, on Wednesday, the first clue that WAT might breakout came with a 5,000 share bid at 63 11/16 (11:35am EST). Shortly thereafter (12:08pm EST), a substantial size bid appears for 10,000 shares at 63 13/16. Instead of running away, WAT goes sideways. I get nervous and raise my protective stop to 63 ¾, just below the prior size bid. However, at 1:40pm a large block of 103,000 shares trades on an up tick (a positive sign) at 64 1/4. At 2:10pm EST, a substantial bidder shows up with 25,000 to buy at 64 1/2, nothing comes his way. At 3:34pm EST, he reappears again with the same 25,000 bid at 64 1/2. Now, he's getting anxious as it's getting late in the trading session – he raises his bid immediately to 64 3/4, I smell blood. A minute later, he raises the bid to 64 7/8, then quickly to 65, then immediately to 65 3/8 and I sense WAT will go out on its high. What's interesting is that the buyer was unable to fill as there was still a 25,000 share bid at the close. Moreover, WAT's action on Wednesday leaves us with a multiple buy signal, it is an Expansion Breakout (new 60 day high on a range greater than any of the last ten) and an Expansion Pivot (as Tuesday the stock traded at it's 50 day moving average). Looking for size to buy near new 60 day highs will often help you anticipate Expansion Breakouts.

GAP RULE: Any buy recommendation that opens 3/4 point above the stated entry price and any sell recommendation that opens 3/4 point below the stated entry price should be ignored for the day.

Reminder...A signal is not valid unless it trades at or above the entry price for buys and at or below the entry price for short sales

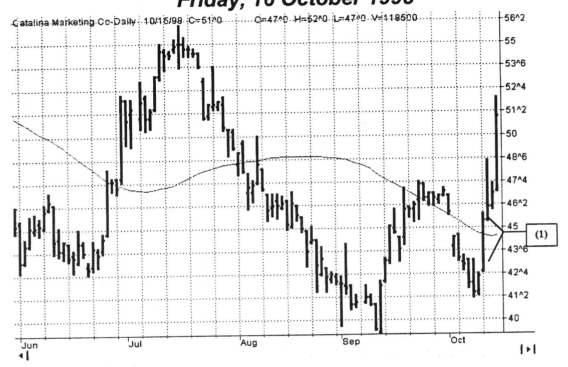

COOPER TRADING INC.
DAILY LEARNING SHEET
Friday, 16 October 1998

Catalina Marketing Co-Daily 10/15/98 C=51^0   O=47^0 H=52^0 L=47^0 V=118500

Multiple Signals With Next Day Stepping In Front Of Size (SIFOS)

Let's take a look at how I select set-ups. Obviously, there are usually many set-ups every evening. How do I differentiate? One of the characteristics I seek out in a solid set-up is an expansion of range that indicates buyers have overwhelmed sellers (for buys). Of course, you don't always get immediate follow though after the momentum of an initial impulse or surge. It's often the "tale" of the pullback or consolidation that reveals much about a stock's direction. The behavior of a stock "post-surge" is a good time to take a stock's temperature. Let's look at an example. POS exploded off a test of lows on October 12 and 13. **(1)** Profit takers hit the stock late on the 13th, leaving a large tail and giving the appearance of a failed breakout. However, the stock held it's own on the 14th creating a multiple buy signal (Jack-In-The-Box/180, shown on Thursday's fax).

We already had over a 2-point profit in POS on Thursday when a substantial bid for 10,000 shares at 50 showed up at 2:29pm EST. This is an indication to add to your position. (Substantial size means we are not waiting for the stock to be bid the uptick.) The bid was raised to 50 1/2 for 5,000 shares at 2:32pm EST. At 2:40pm EST, the buyer steps up to 50 7/8 for 5,000 shares. Nothing is coming in, he's getting nervous. At 2:42pm EST a 10,000 share buyer shows up at 51, at 2:50pm EST. POS trades up to 52 where 6,000 shares changed hands -- finally, the anxious buyer found a level where sellers would supply some inventory. Keep this behavior in mind (a level where supply was offered) as this put a lid on the stock for the balance of the session despite a 250 point last hour Dow rally. At least partial profits should have been taken between 51 and 52. I hope you all participated in the move. As you can see, signals followed by Stepping in Front Of Size (SIFOS) is a powerful tool for creating quick profits. Tonight, POS is an Expansion Breakout. Let's see if the buyer (a trapped short perhaps) returns again Friday.

COOPER TRADING INC.
DAILY LEARNING SHEET
Tuesday, 13 October 1998

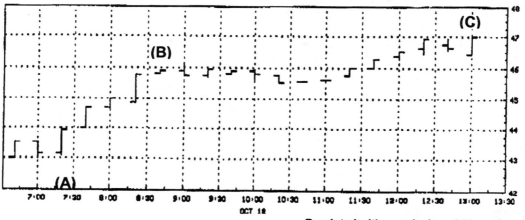

Reprinted with permission of Bloomberg LLP

Putting The Pieces Together: Stepping In Front Of Size (SIFOS) on a Multiple Set-Up

I showed SBL as a multiple buy set-up with a size buyer near the close for Monday. Today it provided a great SIFOS example as the buyer(s) returned (all times EST):

10:22 a bid for 4,700 at 43 1/16 (just shy of 5,000 but enough to consider)
10:23 a bid for 5,800 at 43 3/16 (bid raised creating a SIFOS buy)
10:25 a bid for 5,000 at 43 1/2 (bid raised again, creating another SIFOS buy)
10:27 a bid for 9,800 at 43 3/4 (substantial size, creating a SIFOS: Stepping In Front Of Substantial Size buy and bid raised creating another SIFOS buy)

The stock exploded 3 points higher (B) soon after the first size bid was placed (A). Then after drifting sideways for a few hours, the stock went on to gain another point and close on its high (C). As you can see, on top of a multiple setup with a size buyer near the previous close, we had several SIFOS opportunities intra-day. All of the above pieces help to weight the odds overwhelmingly in your favor. This is how you create extraordinary gains.

COOPER TRADING INC.
DAILY LEARNING SHEET
26 June 1998

REPRINTED WITH PERMISSION OF OMEGA RESEARCH INC.
Chart created using Omega SuperCharts 4.0.

Multiple Set-Up With Size To Buy

In spite of Wednesday's reversal, SDG (an Old friend that many subscribers have had good fortune with), held its gains and closed on its high leaving us with a multiple Expansion Pivot/180 buy set-up with size buyers on the close. Good trading tone relative to overall market performance is an important tool to use in gauging a set-up: stocks often tip their hand to an explosion or breakout in this manner.

As you can see from the above chart, breakouts by SDG are typically characterized by strong momentum spurts (A). This is particularly common in small cap stocks. Why? Because once an institution makes a commitment to own a thin issue, they must buy enough stock to warrant their efforts to follow the company. This translates into a persistent move.

Another piece that makes the picture interesting is the breakout of a triangle formation by SDG. One of the simplest and effective tools is a trend line. Don't ignore them because they may not seem like the most sophisticated indicator. Keeping things simple will allow you to focus. Focus is an important key to enhancing performance in the frenetic trading environment.

COOPER TRADING INC.
DAILY LEARNING SHEET
23 April 1998

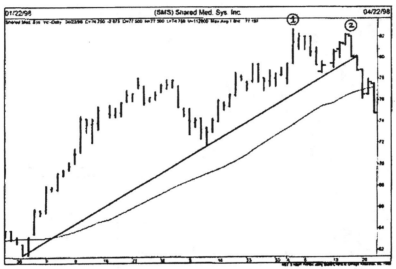

Multiple Set-up With Size for Sale

Here's an interesting short sale set-up for Wednesday. SMS has an Expansion Pivot/180 multiple signal as well as size for sale near the close.

Breaking below the little Flat Top Expansion Breakout from 4/2   after a "return rally" failed on 4/15   leaves us with a picture that looks like distribution: When a stock does what it shouldn't do or goes where it shouldn't go, it is speaking.

By putting these kinds of bigger picture pieces together with Tuesday's shorter-term pieces, we can gain an edge in our trading.

COOPER TRADING, INC.
DAILY LEARNING SHEET
12 NOVEMBER 1997

Petroleum Geo-Services (PGO)

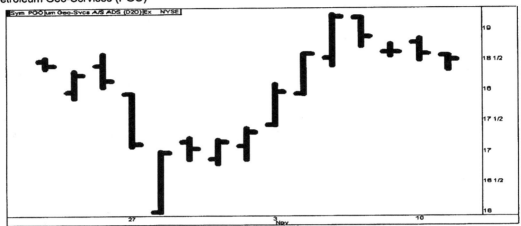

Time	E	Bid/Trd/Ask	E	Size	Time	E	Bid/Trd/Ask	E	Size
13:02	M	$73\frac{3}{4}/74\frac{1}{4}$	P	1X1	12:22	N	$73\frac{1}{2}$		10
13:02	X	$73\frac{3}{4}/74\frac{1}{8}$	M	1X1	12:20	N	$73\frac{3}{8}/73\frac{1}{2}$	N	100X5
13:02	M	$73\frac{3}{4}/74\frac{1}{8}$	M	1X1	**12:15**	**N**	**$73\frac{3}{8}/73\frac{1}{2}$**	**N**	**100X10**
13:02	N	74		80	12:13	N	$73\frac{1}{4}/73\frac{1}{2}$	N	5X10
12:58	**N**	**$73\frac{7}{8}/74$**	**X**	**80X10**	12:11	N	$73\frac{1}{4}/73\frac{1}{2}$	N	5X5
12:58	N	↑$73\frac{7}{8}$	M	20	12:11	N	$73\frac{3}{8}/73\frac{5}{8}$	N	5X5
12:55	N	$73\frac{3}{4}/73\frac{7}{8}$		9X10	12:11	N	↑$73\frac{1}{2}$		5
12:55	N	$73\frac{3}{4}$		1	12:11	N	$73\frac{5}{16}/73\frac{1}{2}$	N	2X10
12:48	N	$73\frac{3}{4}/73\frac{7}{8}$	N	10X10	12:11	N	↑$73\frac{7}{16}$		20
12:48	N	↑$73\frac{3}{4}$	N	10	12:11	N	$73\frac{5}{16}/73\frac{7}{16}$	N	2X10
12:28	N	$73\frac{1}{2}/73\frac{3}{4}$	N	100X10	12:11	N	$73\frac{3}{8}$		3
12:28	**N**	**$73\frac{1}{2}/73\frac{5}{8}$**		**100X10**	12:11	N	↓$73\frac{3}{8}$		3
12:26	N	$73\frac{1}{2}/73\frac{5}{8}$		40X10	12:09	N	$73\frac{3}{8}/73\frac{9}{16}$	N	2X10
12:24	N	$73\frac{7}{16}/73\frac{5}{8}$	N	50X10	12:09	N	$73\frac{1}{2}$		3
12:24	N	$73\frac{1}{2}$	N	5	12:09	N	$73\frac{3}{8}/73\frac{9}{16}$	N	2X5
12:24	N	$73\frac{1}{2}/73\frac{5}{8}$		5X10	12:09	N	↓$73\frac{1}{2}$		3
12:23	**N**	**$73\frac{7}{16}/73\frac{5}{8}$**		**50X10**	12:06	M	↓$73\frac{5}{8}$		2
12:22	N	$73\frac{1}{2}$	N	10	12:06	M	↑$73\frac{3}{4}$		2

Here is an interesting set-up for Wednesday. PGO (Petroleum Geo-Services) has a 1-2-3-4 buy set-up, is almost a 180, and as you can see from the numbers above, had a persistent large buyer aggressively bidding for stock in the last hour of trading.

As I always state, no promises, but if this buyer re-appears, he can easily push this stock higher as it tends to trade thin.

COOPER TRADING INC.
DAILY LEARNING SHEET
30 JANUARY 1998

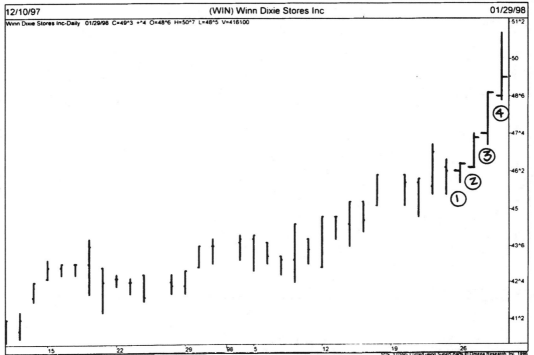

| 12/10/97 | (WIN) Winn Dixie Stores Inc | 01/29/98 |

Winn Dixie Stores Inc-Daily 01/29/98 C=49^3 +^4 O=48^6 H=50^7 L=48^5 V=416100

REPRINTED WITH PERMISSION OF Omega Research Inc.
Chart created using SuperCharts 4.0.

Maximizing Signals, Maximizing Profits

On the sheet dated Tuesday, January 27, we had a Boomer buy set-up on WIN ① (on our Hit List). The signal triggered at 46 1/2 on Tuesday and closed near the high at 47 5/16 (stay long).②

A second reason for carrying the position over was the oversold Cooper Trading Indicator reading of 2 - 3: When a stock closes at a new high and the market is oversold, there is a good chance for a larger than normal move the next day. As you can see, WIN exploded on Wednesday leaving us with a new buy signal (Expansion Breakout).③ The new signal and good close was an indication to keep at least a partial position. Thursday, WIN followed through strongly before coming in ④ -- this is a good example of how trailing stops will protect the lion's share of your profits. After three strong days, you must be extra attentive to tightening up protective stops.

COOPER TRADING INC.
DAILY LEARNING SHEET
Thursday, 1 April 1999

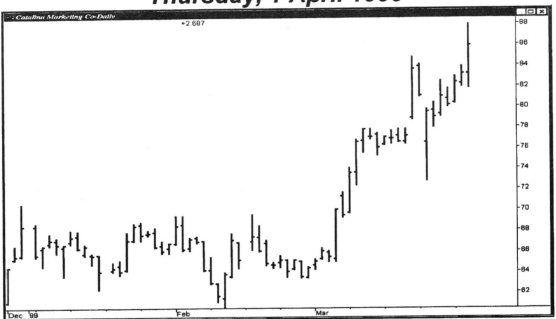

REPRINTED WITH PERMISSION OF OMEGA RESEARCH INC.
Charts created using Omega Super Charts 4.0.

Putting Pieces Together
Anatomy of a Trade

Putting pieces together, trading multiple signals, combining bigger picture patterns with shorter term set-ups or combining two different strategies such as stepping in front of size and intraday Relative Strength, almost always gives you a trading edge.

POS (on your small cap uptrending sheet) had a size offer of 11,000 shares at 81 5/10 knocked out almost immediately after being shown at 9:37 (EST). This was a sign of buying interest. The buyer's appettite has only whetted, as at 10:13 (EST) our friend shows up with a bid for 5,000 at 83. This is our sign to buy; when size offers are taken and soon thereafter size is bid the uptick, in my experience, the stock is a buy at the market (i.e. it is not necessary to wait for an additional size bid). In spite of the market's early rally exhausting itself and reversing, POS held its ground trading up to 84 and creating an outside day. When another size bid for 5,000 shares shows up at 84 5/8 (11:12 EST) POS is on its way to reversal new high signal. Then, at 11:22 a 5,000 size offer at 86 is knocked out. Within 40 minutes POS trades up to 87 7/8. A trailing stop at 87 to 87 1/4 locked in a solid gain of APX 3 1/2 points!

Remember, stocks in a strong trend with good Intraday Relative Strength that show size bids (or offer K.O'S) are saying; "damn the torpedoes, full steam ahead."

COOPER TRADING INC.
DAILY LEARNING SHEET
Monday, 25 January 1999

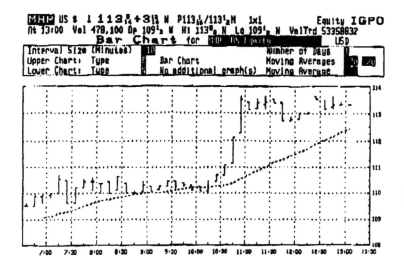

Laurel And Hardys

In a recent learning example, I discussed the concept of stocks having cycles of contraction and expansion of their daily range. The same concept exists intra day. As you can see from the above chart on MHP (on your Hit List), after trading sideways in a tight narrow range all morning (this is a 10 minute bar chart) the stock contracts in an even tighter range for approximately an hour before exploding. What is the tip off?

At 10:14 AM (PST) a size offer of 20,000 shows up. If MHP was going down, one would think that kind of size would have created some nervous selling. Maybe someone was really <u>looking for inventory</u>! Whatever the case, a buyer appears and at 10:23 AM (PST) the size offer was completely knocked out. Another large offer of 10,500 shares shows up at 10:24 AM (PST) and is also quickly knocked out. When size of 10,000 is immediately bid for at 110 3/4 followed by

> 10,000 at 110 7/8
> 5,000 at 111
> 5,000 at 111 5/16
> 10,000 at 111 3/4
> 30,000 at 111 3/4

the stock expands.

Periods of contraction are followed by periods of expansion. This is the natural ebb and flow of volatility whether intra day or in any other time frame. When a leading stock has a thin period of contraction, Stan Laurel, Oliver Hardy may be close behind.

COOPER TRADING INC.
DAILY LEARNING SHEET
Tuesday, 30 March 1999

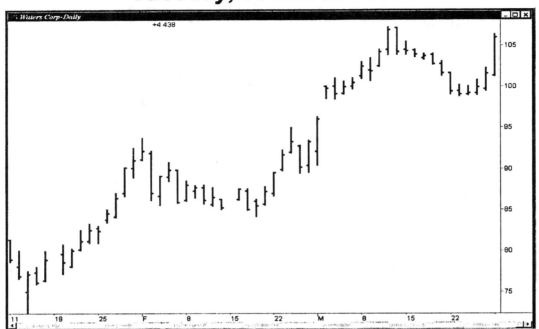

REPRINTED WITH PERMISSION OF OMEGA RESEARCH INC.
Charts created using Omega Super Charts 4.0.

Size Bid/Size Offer Knock Out

One of the best times to stalk stocks for size to buy is after they've pulled back. If an institution could not complete its position during a pullback and the market starts up, there is a better than average likelihood the institution will "step up to the plate" and show, advertise their bid. Such is the case with WAT recommended on Monday's sheet. After pulling back, WAT has a narrow range day (3/23, 3/24) suggesting selling has dried up.

Monday morning, WAT exploded after triggering our set-up (trading above Friday's high) at 102 3/8. At 10:26 (EST) a size bid for 5,000 shares at 103 1/2 appears. The bid is hit. Then, at 10: 46, a size offer of 8,000 shares shows up at 103 1/2. When that offer is knocked out at 11:12 (EST) as 25,000 prints, it is a sign of buying pressure. Although WAT doesn't follow thru immediately, it explodes to 106 3/8 by 1:08 (EST). Not too shabby for 2 hours of patience!

Remember, volume often precedes price. Although we all love immediate gratification, as long as the stock does nothing wrong- it pays to exercise patience as size interest seldom disappears quickly.

COOPER TRADING INC.
DAILY LEARNING SHEET
21 SEPTEMBER 1998

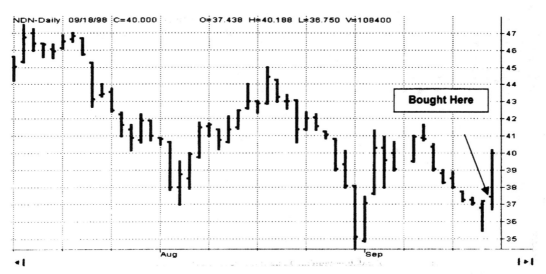

REPRINTED WITH PERMISSION OF OMEGA RESEARCH INC.
Chart created using Omega SuperCharts 4.0.

Size Offer Knockouts: NDN Revisited

The Learning Sheet for Friday showed the Lizard buy set-up on NDN. I also mentioned that the signal was interesting because it was occurring from a level that appeared to be a successful test of recent reaction lows. Remember, daily signals don't exist in a vacuum; it's important to consider the trading context in which they take place. For example: Is the stock testing a swing low or a swing high and succeeding or failing? Is there an underlying bigger picture pattern that may create an edge? Is the stock trending up (higher highs and higher lows or vice versa for down trending stocks) or just chopping back and forth (reducing the likelihood for a meaningful move)? These are some of the questions that I ask myself when focusing on the best set-ups.

When reading stocks, after pattern analysis, in my view, the second most important criteria is that of size. Size bids and offers go a long way in tipping you off to the urgency and agenda of buyers/sellers. Let's take a look at how size played itself out in the NDN set-up. As you know, the stock went out with substantial size to buy Thursday night. After popping open Friday morning, NDN pulls back a little, a normal expectation. However, at 10:43am, a large offer of 14,000 shares at 37 1/4 is swooped up. In all probability, the same buyer from late Thursday returns after letting the stock "soak" for an hour. This is your clue that the set-up is going to work. Again, at 12:27pm, a size offer of 5000 shares at 37 3/4 is taken, further indication of solid buying pressure. Now, the stock is on its way and closes up almost 3 points, giving us a solid gain. I hope you all participated in the move.

COOPER TRADING INC.
DAILY LEARNING SHEET
25 AUGUST 1998

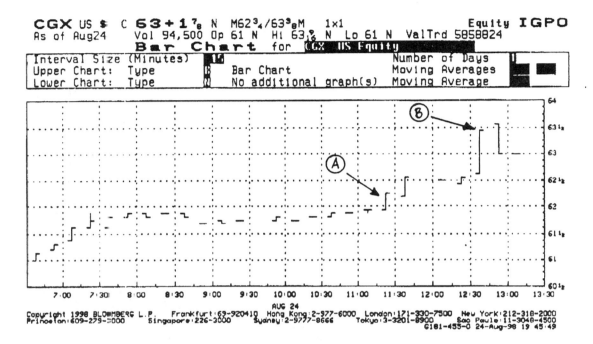

Stepping In Front Of Size: Substantial Size Offered and Taken

CGX, a stock on our Hit List and shown as a 1-2-3-4/Extended Level Boomer for today (Monday) provided a great example of a twist on the Stepping In Front Of Size (SIFOS) methodology. At 2:16pm EST someone took a substantial offer of 10,000 shares at the ask price of 62 (A). The fact that someone paid the offer on such a large block of a thinly traded stock suggests that they were eager to own it and may be looking for more. Soon after the buyer stepped up to the plate, the stock began to rally over 1 ½ points (B) before settling down to close 1 point higher than where the buyer entered. As you can see, its important to pay attention whenever you see substantial size (10,000) taken on a thinly traded stock. Furthermore, when you combine it with multiple set-ups, you will increase your odds of success.

COOPER TRADING INC.
DAILY LEARNING SHEET
APRIL 1 1998

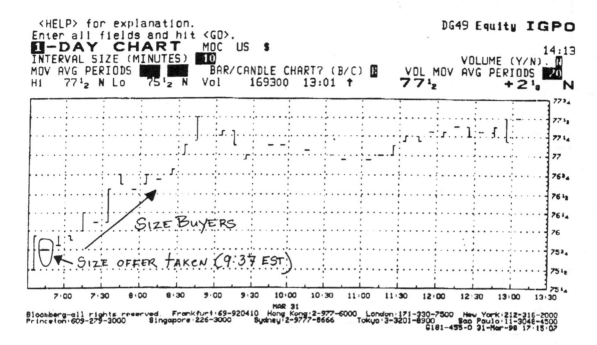

<HELP> for explanation.   DG49 Equity **IGPO**
Enter all fields and hit <GO>.
1-DAY CHART   MOC US $ 14:13
INTERVAL SIZE (MINUTES) **10**   VOLUME (Y/N). **N**
MOV AVG PERIODS ▉ ▉   BAR/CANDLE CHART? (B/C) **B**   VOL MOV AVG PERIODS **20**
HI 77½ N Lo 75½ N Vol   169300 13:01 ↑   **77½**   **+2⅛** N

SIZE BUYERS

SIZE OFFER TAKEN (9:37 EST)

Size Offers Taken/Size Buyers on the Bid

MOC, a stock on our Hit List, provided an excellent example of Stepping in Front of Size today (3/31/98) with size offers taken and buyers on the bid side.

The time and sales were as follows (in Eastern Standard Time):

09:37 Size offered: 13,000 shares, quickly taken by eager buyers
09:50 5,000 shares bid for at 75 13/16
10:04 5,000 shares bid for at 75 7/8 (bid raised)
10:14 5,000 shares bid for at 76 (bid raised again)
10:50 7,300 shares bid for at 76 1/2(bid raised again)

MOC goes on to close the day up 2 1/8 points at 77 ½.

When a size offer (in this case 13,000 shares) is taken out and buyers enter the market and begin bidding up the stock, it creates an excellent opportunity for Stepping in Front of Size.

COOPER TRADING INC.
DAILY LEARNING SHEET
29 JANUARY 1998

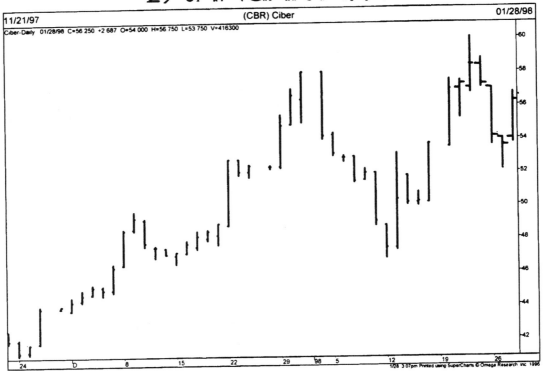

| 11/21/97 | (CBR) Ciber | 01/28/98 |

Ciber-Daily 01/28/98 C=56.250 +2.687 O=54.000 H=56.750 L=53.750 V=416300

REPRINTED WITH PERMISSION OF Omega Research Inc.
Chart created using SuperCharts 4.0.

Taking Out Size Offers

Last night's sheet showed a 1-2-3-4 buy on CBR which triggered at 54 1/8. Wednesday, the tip-off that the trade was going to work came when a size offer of 10,000 shares at 54 1/4 (11:13am EST) was taken out. Again at 12:19pm EST, a size offer of 20,000 shares at 54 9/16 was lifted. This further confirmed the underlying demand and gave us an indication to double up on our position. At 12:31pm EST, another large offer (17,000 shares at 54 3/4) is taken, further validating the up move.

Size offers removed (bought) on small cap relatively thinly traded stocks reflects a large appetite on the part of buyers; this is a twist to our Stepping In Front Of Size (on the bid) strategy.

COOPER TRADING INC.
DAILY LEARNING SHEET
Monday, 07 December 1998

Jefferson Pilot Corp-Daily   12/04/98   C=71.000   +2.562   O=68.438

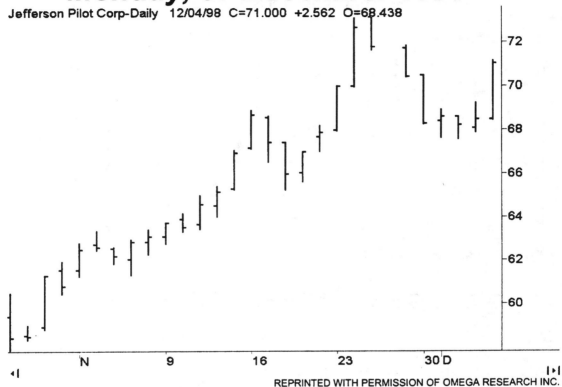

REPRINTED WITH PERMISSION OF OMEGA RESEARCH INC.
Chart created using Omega SuperCharts 4.0.

Size Offer Knockouts

Sometimes a size offer knocked out can be a bigger tip off to a momentum move than size to buy. This is because often institutions don't show the world their intentions. Often they will work an order discreetly or give a large order to a broker to work in the crowd. You can't always depend upon your screen to advertise precisely what's in the market at any given time. Institutions prefer to be patient (given the chance) and usually don't have to chase a stock.

The unstated methodology of many large institutions for accumulating a position in a desired stock is to buy pullbacks. This is why, when you see size taken, it is a very strong clue of a momentum move to follow.

Let's take a look at the V-Thrust set on JP we had for Friday. The 5,000 share offer at 69 1/4 knocked out at 10:41EST was a good sign that the set-up would work. The substantial size offer of 10,000 shares taken at 11:46 EST at 69 1/2 was further confirmation. Size offer knockouts are a true and real indication of underlying demand.

Charts created using SuperCharts® by Omega Research, Inc.   Copyright @ 1998, Cooper Trading, Inc.
Past results are not indicative of future returns. There is a high degree of risk in trading. Cooper Trading Inc. assumes no responsibility for your trading results. Principals of Cooper Trading Inc. may at times maintain directly or indirectly positions mentioned in this service.

COOPER TRADING, INC.
DAILY LEARNING SHEET
21 OCTOBER 1997

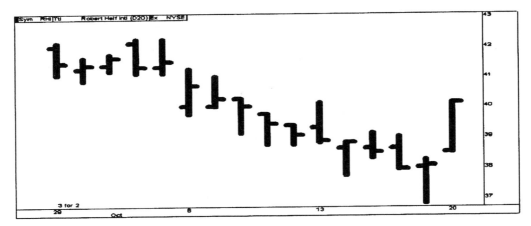

ROBERT HALF INTL INC (RHI)

Time	E	Bid/Trd/Ask	E	Size	Time	E	Bid/Trd/Ask	E	Size
13:33	P	$39\,^9/_{16}/40\,^{11}/_{16}$	P	1x1	12:49	N	$\uparrow40$		2
13:18	M	$39\,^7/_8/40\,^3/_8$	M	1x1	12:49	T	$\downarrow39\,^{15}/_{16}$		2
13:00	X	$40/40\,^3/_8$	M	1x1	12:48	N	$39\,^{15}/_{16}/40\,^1/_{16}$	N	10X20
13:00	T	$40\,^1/_8$		31	12:48	N	$39\,^{15}/_{16}/40\,^1/_{16}$	N	10X2
13:00	X	$39\,^7/_8/40\,^3/_8$	X	1X1	12:48	N	$\uparrow40\,^1/_{16}$		10
13:00	M	$39\,^7/_8/40\,^1/_4$	M	1X1	12:46	N	$39\,^{15}/_{16}/40\,^1/_8$	N	10X21
13:00	N	$40\,^1/_8$		35	12:46	N	$39\,^{15}/_{16}/40\,^1/_8$	N	10X6
13:00	N	$\uparrow40\,^1/_8$		6	12:46	N	$39\,^{15}/_{16}/40\,^1/_{16}$	N	10X10
12:59	N	$40/40\,^1/_8$	N	50X10	12:46	N	$39\,^7/_8/40\,^1/_{16}$	N	10X10
12:54	N	$40/40\,^1/_{16}$	N	50X7	12:46	N	$\downarrow39\,^{15}/_{16}$		2
12:52	N	$40/40\,^1/_{16}$	N	50X5	12:45	N	$39\,^7/_8/40$	N	10X5
12:52	N	$40\,^1/_{16}$		10	12:45	N	40		10
12:52	M	$40\,^1/_{16}$		10	12:45	P	$\uparrow40$		10
12:52	N	$40/40\,^1/_{16}$	N	50X15	12:43	N	$39\,^7/_8/40$	N	10X15
12:52	N	$40/40\,^1/_{16}$	N	45X15	12:43	N	$39\,^7/_8/40\,^1/_{16}$	N	10X10
12:52	N	$40\,^1/_{16}$		5	12:43	N	$\downarrow39\,^{15}/_{16}$		14
12:51	M	$\uparrow40\,^1/_{16}$		5	12:41	N	$39\,^7/_8/40$	N	10X5
12:49	M	$40/40\,^1/_{16}$	N	45X20	12:41	N	$\uparrow40$		50

Chart created using Qcharts by Quote.com, Inc.
© 1999 by Quote.com

RHI (Robert Half Int'l) is a stock which has treated me well in the past. For Tuesday we have an Expansion Pivot buy and a buyer left over (at 40) from Monday's close. Watch to see if the buyer re-appears to help trigger our signal.

COOPER TRADING INC.
DAILY LEARNING SHEET
Tuesday, 27 April 1999

Ethan Allen Interiors Inc-Daily   04/26/99 C=50.875 +1.625 O=49.187 H=51.500 L=49.125

Size to Buy on Pullbacks

Although ETH has not been trending long enough over time to create an ADX reading __ greater than 30, the stock has surged since recapturing its 50 day Moving Average and late last week encountered its first pullback.

First pullbacks after strong impulses offer solid risk to reward set-ups. Friday's close left ETH with a 1-2-3-4 low close set up. In my experience, don't ignore pullbacks that close poorly; A low tick close multiday pullback in a strong trend often indicates the selling is dried up and near complete and that hot money is flushed out, leaving the rubber band pulled back and the stock ripe for a snap back.

The key is follow thru. If they're not going lower after 3 to 4 days against the main trend, the underlying trend may be ready to reassert itself! This is a good time to stalk the stock for size to buy as institutions prefer to add/enter a position on pullbacks (when given an opportunity).

So what happens? At 9:41 (EST) 5,000 shares is offered at 49 1/4. At first glance it appeared that last week's selling would continue. However, the stock holds and the offer is taken at 10:03 (EST). At 10:24 (EST) ETH is bid the up tick and although the stock didn't explode immediately, 2 hours later ETH was up more than 2 points at 51 ½.

While many NASDAQ stocks offer some magnificent intraday moves, their greater rewards come with larger risk as the intraday noise inherent in these names makes tape reading difficult. Don't forget to capitalize on the Stepping in Front of Size Strategy on NYSE stocks.

COOPER TRADING INC.
DAILY LEARNING SHEET
4 FEBRUARY 1998

Equity Q R M

Screen printed.

M A R K E T / T R A D E   R E C A P   Page 1
Volumes scaled by 100

Time ▓:▓   Min Vol ▓▓100
Date ▓/▓   Price Range ▓▓▓▓ To ▓▓▓▓

COMDISCO INC   (CDO   US)   PRICE 39³₈   N $

Time	E	Bid/Trd/Ask	E	Size	Cond	Time	E	Bid/Trd/Ask	E	Size	Cond
13:18	P	39³₁₆/39⁹₁₆	P	5x5		12:56	T	39¹₄/39⁷₁₆	N	1x2	TRIM
13:05	X	39¹₄/39⁹₁₆	P	1x5		12:56	N	↓39¹₄		45	
13:03	X	39¹₄/39⁵₈	M	1x1		12:56	N	39¹₄/39⁷₁₆	N	23x2	
13:01	X	39¹₄/39¹₂	B	1x1		12:56	X	39⁵₁₆/39⁷₁₆	N	1x2	
13:00	N	39³₈		19		12:56	N	↓39⁵₁₆		5	
13:00	N	39³₈		5		12:54	N	39³₈		8	
13:00	X	39¹₄/39³₈	T	1x1	TRIM	12:54	N	39³₈		5	
13:00	X	39¹₄/39³₈	T	1x1	TRIM	12:53	N	39³₈		2	
13:00	N	39³₈		37		12:52	N	39⁵₁₆/39⁷₁₆	N	5x2	
13:00	N	↑39³₈		110		12:52	N	39³₈		4	
13:00	N	39¹₄/39³₈	N	19x37		12:51	N	39⁵₁₆/39⁷₁₆	N	5x6	
12:59	N	↑39⁵₁₆		4		12:51	N	39⁵₁₆/39³₈	T	5x1	TRIM
12:59	N	39¹₄/39⁵₁₆	N	19x4		12:51	N	39³₈		6	
12:57	N	39³₁₆/39⁵₁₆	N	55x4		12:51	N	39⁵₁₆/39³₈	N	5x6	
12:57	N	39³₁₆/39⁵₁₆	N	50x4		12:50	N	39³₈		3	
12:56	N	39³₁₆/39⁵₁₆	N	50x3		12:50	N	39³₈		5	
12:56	T	39¹₄/39⁵₁₆	N	1x3	TRIM	12:50	N	39³₈		2	
12:56	T	39¹₄/39³₈	N	1x3	TRIM	12:49	N	39³₈		10	

Bloomberg-all rights reserved. Frankfurt:69-920410 Hong Kong:2-521-3000 London:171-330-7500 New York:212-318-2000
Princeton:609-279-3000   Singapore:226-3000   Sydney:2-9777-8600   Tokyo:3-3201-8900   Sao Paulo:11 3048-4500
Q181-455-0 03-Feb 98 18:54:51

REPRINTED WITH PERMISSION OF BLOOMBERG L.P.

Comdisco (CDO), a technology consulting and leasing company, has an Expansion Breakout buy for Wednesday. What is also intriguing is that the stock had persistent buyers throughout the day. In fact, as you can see, these buyers were still bidding for stock on the close.

Should these buyers again show their hand in the morning, the stock could easily move higher.

COOPER TRADING INC.
DAILY LEARNING SHEET
20 OCTOBER 1997

QRM
Screen printed.

DG49 **Equity Q R M**

M A R K E T / T R A D E   R E C A P   Volumes scaled by 100   Page 1

Time ▓▓:▓▓   Min Vol ▓▓▓**100**
Date **10/17**   Price Range ▓▓▓▓▓   To ▓▓▓▓▓

SOUTHDOWN INC   (SDW   US)   PRICE 54^9 $_{16}$ N $

Time	E	Bid/Trd/Ask	E	Size	Cond	Time	E	Bid/Trd/Ask	E	Size	Cond
13:17	P	54^9 $_{16}$/54^{11} $_{16}$	P	9x2		12:41	N	54^7 $_{16}$/54^5 $_8$	N	6x5	
13:08	P	54^5 $_{16}$/54^{11} $_{16}$	P	2x2		12:41	N	54^3 $_8$/54^5 $_8$	N	5x5	
13:04	N	54^9 $_{16}$		34	*C	12:40	N	↓54^1 $_2$		3	
13:04	N	54^9 $_{16}$		34	*X	12:40	T	↑54^9 $_{16}$		3	
13:01	M	54^1 $_4$/54^3 $_4$	M	1x1		12:38	N	54^3 $_8$/54^5 $_8$	N	20x10	
13:01	T	54^5 $_{16}$/54^3 $_4$	T	5x5	TRIM	12:36	N	↑54^1 $_2$		117	
13:01	N	↑54^9 $_{16}$		2		12:33	N	54^7 $_{16}$/54^5 $_8$	N	20x10	
12:58	N	54^3 $_8$/54^5 $_8$	N	50x38		12:32	N	54^7 $_{16}$/54^9 $_{16}$	P	20x1	
12:57	N	54^3 $_8$/54^5 $_8$	N	50x18		12:32	N	54^7 $_{16}$/54^9 $_{16}$	P	20x1	
12:55	N	54^3 $_8$/54^5 $_8$	N	20x18		12:31	T	↓54^3 $_8$		1	
12:46	N	↓54^1 $_2$		1		12:31	N	↑54^1 $_2$		5	
12:44	N	54^3 $_8$/54^5 $_8$	N	5x5		12:31	N	↑54^3 $_8$		1	
12:44	N	54^3 $_8$/54^5 $_8$	T	5x5	TRIM	12:30	N	54^1 $_4$/54^1 $_2$	N	50x5	
12:44	N	54^3 $_8$/54^5 $_8$	N	10x10		12:30	N	54^1 $_4$/54^1 $_2$	N	50x10	
12:44	N	54^9 $_{16}$		10		12:30	N	54^1 $_8$/54^1 $_2$	N	30x10	
12:43	N	54^3 $_8$/54^9 $_{16}$	N	10x10		12:29	X	54^1 $_4$		1	
12:42	N	54^7 $_{16}$/54^9 $_{16}$	N	10x10		12:28	N	54^1 $_8$/54^3 $_8$	N	30x10	
12:42	N	↑54^9 $_{16}$		10		12:28		/54^3 $_8$	N	x10	

A Stock To Watch For Monday

Southdown (SDW) is a cement manufacturer with a strongly uptrending chart pattern. On Friday, in spite of the massive stock market sell-off, this stock did not go down, leaving us with an HG2 buy set-up. What makes it even more intriguing is that in the last hour, a large buyer showed up looking for stock at 54, then 54 1/8, 54 1/4 and finally at 54 3/8. Should he and the other buyers come back on Monday, we could possibly see the stock make new highs.

COOPER TRADING INC.
DAILY LEARNING SHEET
31 MARCH 1998

REPRINTED WITH PERMISSION OF Omega Research Inc.
Chart created using Omega SuperCharts 4.0.

Carrying a Position Overnight/Size Buyer

On Friday (3/27/98) we showed SDG as a 1-2-3-4 buy. The stock gapped open then rallied strongly all day to close over 2 points higher and near the day's highs. When a stock closes strongly, especially in a sloppy overall market, it's a good idea to carry a piece of the position overnight.* What makes it even more interesting is today's follow-through. The stock opened stronger then formed a base for most of the morning. Then at 12:39 (EST) a massive size buyer enters the market, bidding for 100,000 shares at 80 ¼. The stock then rallies to close over two points higher from the size bid. When a massive buyer bids for a thinly traded stock it creates a tremendous opportunity for Stepping in Front of Size. With an XBO buy signal for tomorrow (3/31/98), it should be interesting to see if the size buyer returns.

*Note: XL (an HG2 buy on 3/27/98) was also a good example of a stock that closed strongly (on 3/27/98) and should have been held overnight.

COOPER TRADING INC.
DAILY LEARNING SHEET
13 APRIL 1998

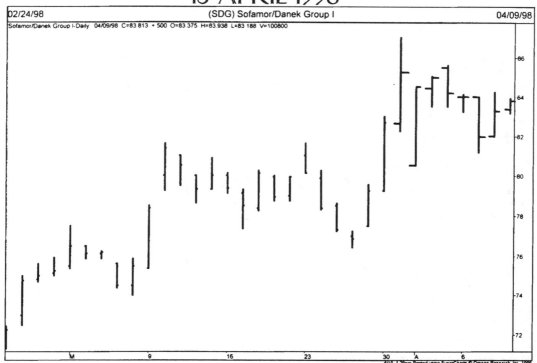

| 02/24/98 | (SDG) Sofamor/Danek Group I | 04/09/98 |

Sofamor/Danek Group I-Daily 04/09/98 C=83.813 + 500 O=83.375 H=83.938 L=83.188 V=100800

Reprinted with permission of Omega Research Inc.
Chart created using Omega SuperCharts 4.0.

Bread And Butter

Stepping In Front Of Size on thinly traded stocks is a bread and butter strategy. I rely heavily on this technique for intraday trading.

When an institution(s) decides to own a relatively thinly traded stock, they must take down size positions or its not worth devoting their resources to follow the company.

When you see a size bid raised (bid the uptick), it means no stock is coming their way and they must step up the price they are willing to pay. Ordinarily, institutions like to buy on pullbacks (if afforded the opportunity) and may not like to chase a stock, so when you do see size bids consistently raised, it is often an indication of urgency on someone's (someone big) part to own the stock.

Urgency to own a stock creates fast moves!

Near Thursday's close, SDG had a size buyer step-up with a bid for 7300 shares at 83 1/2. Minutes later the bid was raised to 83 3/4 for 11,000 shares. The buyer(s) was not filled; and, it will be interesting to see if he reappears Monday morning.

COOPER TRADING INC.
DAILY LEARNING SHEET
10 FEBRUARY 1998

<HELP> for explanation, <MENU> for similar functions.   DG49 **Equity Q R M**
Screen printed.

M A R K E T / T R A D E   R E C A P   Page 1
Volumes scaled by 100

Time ▨:▨   Min Vol ▨ 100
Date 2/9   Price Range ▨   To ▨
BRIGGS & STRATTON   (BGG   US)   PRICE 44⁵₈   N $

Time	E	Bid/Trd/Ask	E	Size	Cond	Time	E	Bid/Trd/Ask	E	Size	Cond
13:33	P	44⁷₁₆/44⁷₈	P	1x1		12:25	N	44³₄		10	
13:03	P	44⁷₁₆/44⁷₈	M	1x1		12:24	N	44³₄		5	
13:01	N	44⁵₈		1		12:23	N	↑44³₄		5	
12:59	N	44⁹₁₆/44³₄	N	29x100 ◄—		12:23	N	44¹¹₁₆/44¹³₁₆	N	50x5	
12:59	N	44⁹₁₆/44³₄	N	10x100		12:09	N	44⁹₁₆/44¹¹₁₆	N	10x5	
12:58	N	44⁹₁₆/44³₄	N	10x45		12:09	N	44¹¹₁₆		1	
12:55	N	44⁹₁₆/44¹¹₁₆	N	10x50		12:06	N	44⁹₁₆/44¹¹₁₆	N	10x1	
12:55	N	44⁹₁₆/44⁷₈	N	10x20		12:05	N	44⁹₁₆/44¹¹₁₆	N	10x2	
12:55	N	↓44⁵₈		6		12:02	N	44⁹₁₆/44¹¹₁₆	N	10x1	
12:45	N	44⁵₈/44⁷₈	N	6x20		12:00	N	44⁹₁₆/44¹¹₁₆	N	10x30	
12:45	N	44⁵₈/44⁷₈	N	6x5		12:00	N	↑44¹¹₁₆		1	
12:44	C	44⁵₈/44⁷₈	N	2x5		11:59	N	44⁹₁₆/44¹¹₁₆	.N	10x1	
12:44	C	44⁵₈/44⁷₈	N	2x5		11:59	N	↓44⁵₈		2	
12:36	N	↑44³₄		3		11:58	N	44⁹₁₆/44¹³₁₆	N	10x32	
12:30	N	44¹¹₁₆/44⁷₈	N	37x5		11:57	N	44⁹₁₆/44¹¹₁₆	N	10x2	
12:30	N	↓44¹¹₁₆		13		11:56	T	↓44¹¹₁₆		1	
12:27	N	44¹¹₁₆/44⁷₈	N	50x5		11:53	N	44⁹₁₆/44¹¹₁₆	N	10x10	
12:27	N	44³₄		5		11:52		/44¹¹₁₆	N	x10	

Briggs and Stratton is a good set-up to look at on Tuesday. The stock has a strongly trending ADX reading of 50 and a 1-2-3-4 sell set-up. Also, as you can see from the arrow above, a large seller arrived late in the day looking to unload some stock.

Please use some caution though because the stock trades thin.

COOPER TRADING INC.
DAILY LEARNING SHEET
31 AUGUST 1998

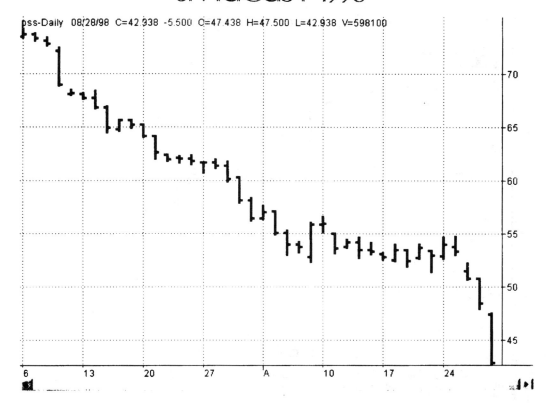

pss-Daily 08/28/98 C=42.938 -5.500 O=47.438 H=47.500 L=42.938 V=598100

How To Recognize When Institutions Throw In The Towel

Size for sale at new lows is often an indication of capitulation. In keeping with last night's example when size for sale is present right off the open (at/near new lows), it many times means an institution has an agenda, that they've thrown in the towel and want out of the stock. Such was the case with PSS (on the Small Cap Hit List) Friday morning as a 5,000 share offer appeared at the open at 47 1/2. Although the first uptick occurred at 46 13/16 and then again at 47 3/16, when a substantial offer of 20,000 shares appeared again at 46 15/16 (10:37am EST), it became apparent that the seller had much more to go and that there was a good likelihood of an Expansion Breakdown in the making. PSS closed down 5 1/2 at 42 15/16. As you can see size for sale at new lows is as powerful an indication of momentum explosions as is size to buy at new highs.

COOPER TRADING, INC.
DAILY LEARNING SHEET
17 OCTOBER 1997

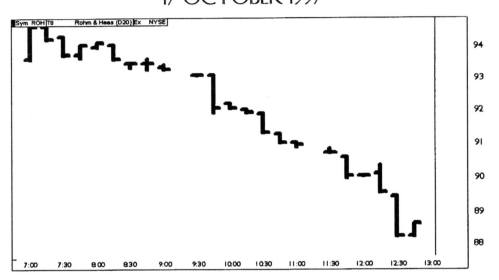

Chart created using Qcharts by Quote.com, Inc.
© 1999 by Quote.com

Stepping in Front of Size on the Downside

ROH, on our Small Cap Downtrend list, is a good example of what can happen to a stock that, already in a downtrend announces somewhat better than expected earnings, and the subsequent morning attempt to rally is viewed as an opportunity to unload stock by big sellers.

It is the classic case of "If they're not going up on good news, they're probably going down."

As I said before, ROH, trading below its 10 and 50 day moving average, was already in a downtrend and therefore in a vulnerable position should someone want to take advantage of the good news to exit a position. This is exactly what occurred Thursday as ROH rallied back up to the area of its prior breakdown (94-95).

Here is what transpired:

7:18 PST	A large seller of 10,000 shares shows up at 94 5/8.
	(3 minutes later the offer is increased to 13,000 shares).
7:26	13,000 shares is offered on a downtick at 94 7/16.
7:27	13,000 shares is offered at 94 5/16.
7:28	The offer is increased to 20,000 shares.

This is an extremely large offer for a thin stock. It's also appearent there is a short seller at work amongst the other sellers (as the offer is continuously lowered). At this point, ROH is a fairly low risk short opportunity.

7:32	6,000 shares shows up for sale at 94 1/8.
7:33	6,000 shares is offered at 94 1/16.
7:34	Again, 6,000 shares is offered at 94.

The first uptick occurs at 7:36 at 93 7/8 and we place a stop at 94 ¾. The stock moves sideways for about a half hour before collapsing.

As you can see, selling often begets more selling and once the stock goes negative, panic sets in creating a wind fall profit.

Section II

PULLBACKS

▪ ▪

Pullback strategies go hand-in-hand with Momentum Trading. In fact, nearly every trade I make comes from a pre-selected group of high momentum stocks which I call the Hit List.

The inherent tendency of these stocks to keep moving in their present direction makes them ideal candidates for the Pullback Strategies described in this section. Just as the most opportune time to catch a moving freight train is when it slows down, my 1-2-3-4 and First Pullback setups allow us to catch pauses that occur just prior to the resumption of powerful trends. Using a stop to risk no more than 1 point, you can make a good living just trading these types of setups.

COOPER TRADING INC.
DAILY LEARNING SHEET
9 MARCH 1998

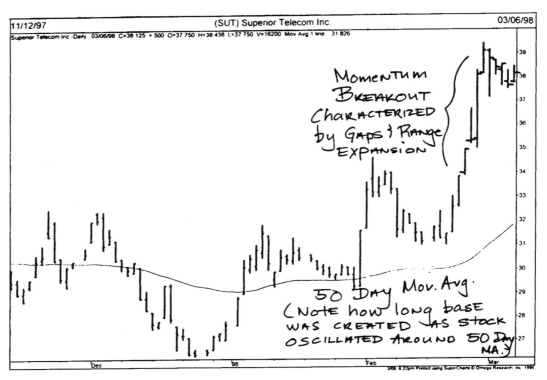

Reprinted with permission of Omega Research Inc.
Chart created using SuperCharts 4.0.

First Pullbacks

As you've heard me say before, First Pullbacks after strong breakouts offer great risk to reward.

When a breakout occurs after a long base has been built creating a strong initial thrust, then the first pullback into the momentum typically offers a solid buying opportunity. This is because stocks don't succumb easily to deep corrections after powerful momentum breakouts occur. The first pullback may take place more in time than price. This allows the stock to work off an overbought condition before continuing in the direction of the dominant trend.

SUT is a good example of an explosion and a tight pullback in price which creates a bullish pennant formation.

COOPER TRADING INC.
DAILY LEARNING SHEET
Tuesday, 10 November 1998

Cigna Corp-Daily   11/09/98   C=75^3   +^2   O=73^2   H=75^6   L=73^2

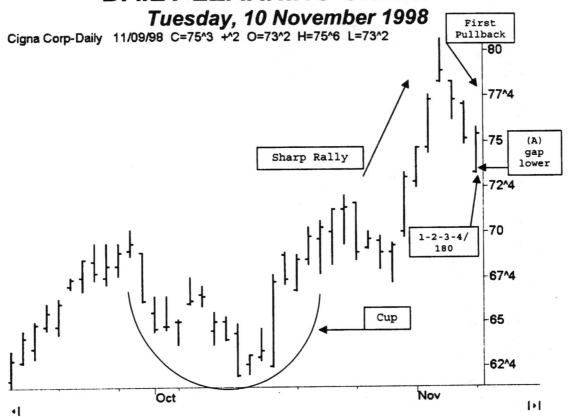

REPRINTED WITH PERMISSION OF OMEGA RESEARCH INC.
Chart created using Omega SuperCharts 4.0.

1-2-3-4/180 Combination On The First Pullback

As many of you know, the 1-2-3-4/180 is one of my favorite multiple set-ups. When it occurs during the first pullback it's even better. Let's look at CI. After breaking out of a cup formation, CI begins to rally sharply. Then in its first pullback it sells off for 2 days and gaps lower on the 3rd day (Monday) (A). However, notice that the gap is right at the low for the day. This suggests that the "scared" money was shaken out on the open and the "smart money" stepped in to accommodate their selling. It then rallys to close near its high to form a multiple Non-ADX 1-2-3-4/180 buy set-up for Tuesday. One other point, notice that it is in the V-Thrusts "position". This means that if it trades above Monday's high on Tuesday it will be a V-Thrust for Wednesday. All of this suggests that CI is poised to resume its up trend.

Look for the 1-2-3-4/180 combination in first pullbacks, especially after bigger picture consolidations (i.e. cups).

COOPER TRADING INC.
DAILY LEARNING SHEET
15 JANUARY 1998

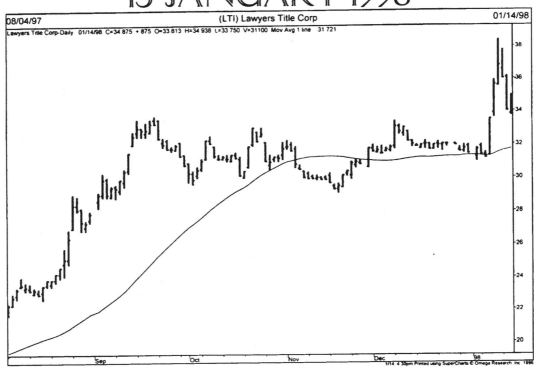

| 08/04/97 | (LTI) Lawyers Title Corp | 01/14/98 |

Lawyers Title Corp-Daily 01/14/98 C=34 875 + 875 O=33.813 H=34 938 L=33 750 V=31100 Mov Avg 1 line   31 721

Signals After First Pullbacks

Here's an interesting set-up for Thursday. LTI has a multiple buy signal -- it is a 1-2-3-4 (the ADX has just popped over 30) as well as a 180.

You can also see that this is the first pullback by LTI since its Expansion Breakout over a flat-top formation on January 7. Signals after first pullbacks from strong breakouts have a very good likelihood of follow through and offer a favorable risk-to-reward.

COOPER TRADING INC. DAILY LEARNING SHEET 9 APRIL 1998

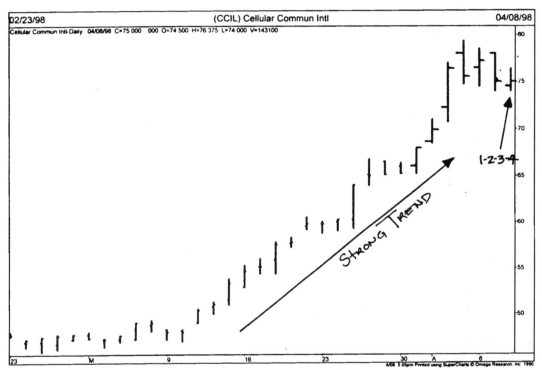

| 02/23/98 | (CCIL) Cellular Commun Intl | 04/08/98 |

Cellular Commun Intl-Daily 04/08/98 C=75 000 000 O=74 500 H=76 375 L=74 000 V=143100

STRONG TREND

1-2-3-4

REPRINTED WITH PERMISSION OF Omega Research Inc.
Chart created using SuperCharts 4.0.

First 1-2-3-4 Signal In A Strong Trend

In a strong trend, it often pays to go with the first pullback signals (BM/HG2/1-2-3-4). CCIL has been trending strongly for the past four weeks. This is confirmed by an ADX reading of nearly 65. Notice that the 1-2-3-4 buy signal (for 4/9/98) is the first 3 day pullback since the stock took off back in mid-March. Should this set-up trigger, it should easily challenge old highs.

COOPER TRADING INC.
DAILY LEARNING SHEET
Thursday, 19 November 1998

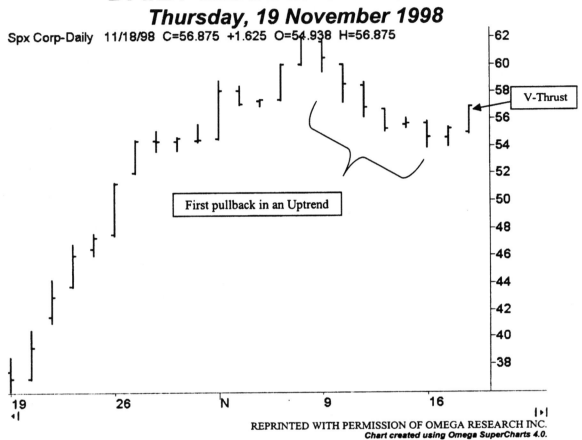

Spx Corp-Daily   11/18/98 C=56.875 +1.625 O=54.938 H=56.875

V-Thrust

First pullback in an Uptrend

First Pullbacks

The V-Thrust strategy does a good job of helping to define when a pullback is over. When a
V-Thrust occurs coming out of a "first pullback" there is a strong likelihood of follow thru.
On Wednesday SPW started to pivot back in the direction of the near term trend, suggesting
that the pullback that allowed the stock to walk off a short-term overbought condition was
complete. Add to the picture a large offer of 7,600 shares (at 56 1/2) knocked out in the last 15
minutes (a 25,000 block traded on an uptick at 56 1/2) and you have the making of a solid buy
candidate for Thursday.

COOPER TRADING INC.
DAILY LEARNING SHEET
30 JUNE 1998

First Pullbacks After A Breakout/Multiple Signals

When looking for buy set-ups, I often look for stocks in long term up trends, first pullbacks after breakouts and of course multiple signals. TWX provides an interesting example. After a long term up trend, the stock consolidates around its 50 day moving average. It attempts to sell off (at (A) and (B)) but quickly reverses to trade back at the average. It then breaks out to the upside. This breakout is characterized by an expansion in the direction of the longer term trend and by gapping open to new highs. Both are very bullish signs. In the first pullback it forms a multiple 180/1-2-3-4 (non-ADX) buy set-up for Tuesday. The combination of a longer term trend, multiple signals and the first pullback after a breakout suggests that TWX could easily challenge its old highs around 89.

COOPER TRADING INC.
DAILY LEARNING SHEET
5 MAY 1998

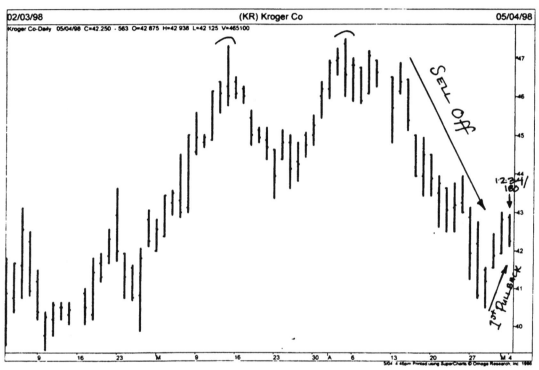

REPRINTED WITH PERMISSION OF OMEGA RESEARCH INC.
Chart created using Omega SuperCharts 4.0.

Combining First Pullbacks with Multiple Signals

After a strong uptrend, KR forms a double top and then proceeds to sell off. In its first pullback it forms a 1-2-3-4/180 multiple sell set-up. As you've heard me say before, first pullbacks after a strong breakdown offer great risk-to-reward. They allow the stock to work off an oversold condition before continuing in the direction of the dominant trend. When you combine a multiple sell set-up along with a first pullback you odds become even greater.

COOPER TRADING, INC.
DAILY LEARNING SHEET
19 NOVEMBER 1997

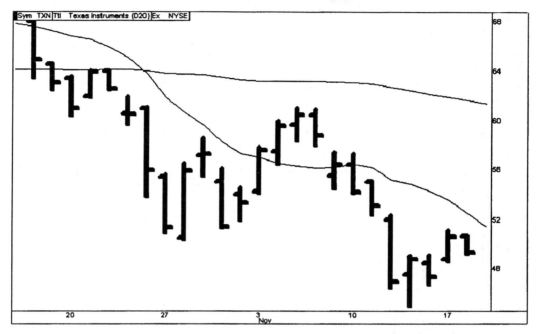

Sym TXN | Ttl Texas Instruments (D20) | Ex NYSE

Chart created using Qcharts by Quote.com, Inc.
© 1999 by Quote.com

For Wednesday, TXN (Texas Instruments) a stock on our Big Cap Hit List, has one of my favorite setups; a 1-2-3-4 combined with a 180.

As you are aware, I am a big advocate of multiple signals. When two independent signals occur together, it increases the likelihood of the trade being a success. My favorite combination is the 1-2-3-4/180. I have had good success over the years trading this setup, especially to the upside (but this setup is to the downside).

As always, no promises, but if you consistently trade this setup, you changes of success will be higher than normal.

COOPER TRADING INC.
DAILY LEARNING SHEET
Tuesday, 15 September 1998

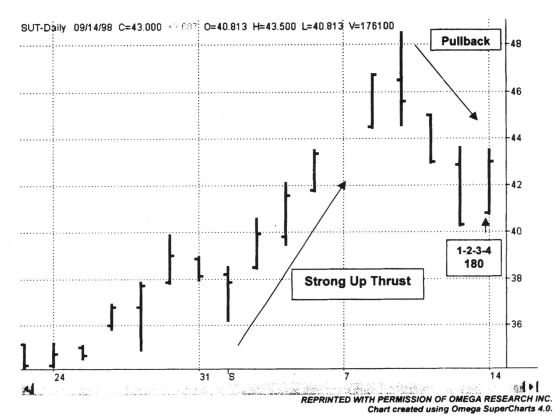

SUT-Daily 09/14/98 C=43.000 O=40.813 H=43.500 L=40.813 V=176100

REPRINTED WITH PERMISSION OF OMEGA RESEARCH INC.
Chart created using Omega SuperCharts 4.0.

1-2-3-4/180

As a general rule (remember there are no EXACT rules in trading) a multiple set-up has a better chance of success than a stand alone set-up. Furthermore, there are certain combinations that tend to work even better. The 1-2-3-4/180 is one of my favorites. The 1-2-3-4 is a good pattern for recognizing a pullback in a strongly trending stock. The 180 is a reversal in the direction of the trend. When combined, you now have a signal that suggests the pullback is complete and the stock is ready to resume its underlying trend. SUT provides an interesting example. After a strong up thrust, SUT consolidates by pulling back. Then today it forms a 1-2-3-4/180 buy set-up for Tuesday. Also of interest is the fact that 18,700 shares of the stock traded on an up tick right near the close. The combination of these factors suggests that SUT will resume its up trend. Let's stalk this one on Tuesday.

COOPER TRADING INC.
DAILY LEARNING SHEET
23 FEBRUARY 1998

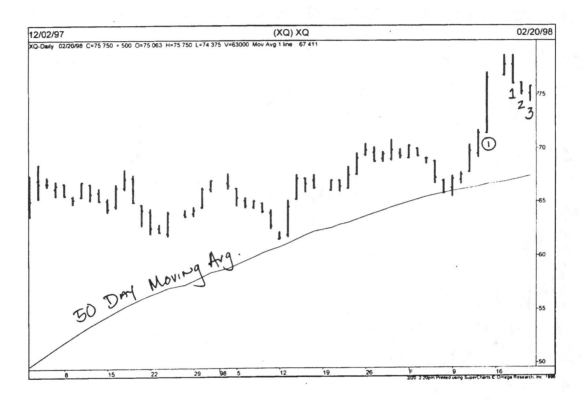

1-2-3-4, 180 Buy

XQ, Quality Foods, in the strong food group, has a multiple signal for Monday. We have a 1-2-3-4, 180 set-up, and as you can see, this is the first pullback into the flat top expansion range breakout (2/13). ① First pullbacks after thrusts over bases offer terrific risk to reward. Friday's 180, as well as the fact that there was a large buyer near the close make a great argument for a continuation of the Breakout to commence now.

COOPER TRADING INC.
LEARNING SHEET
Monday, 07 June 1999

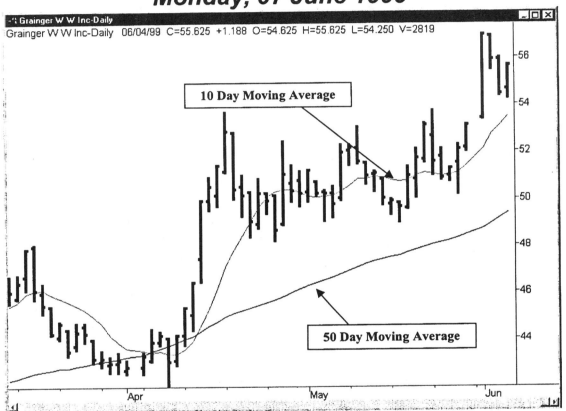

Grainger W W Inc-Daily

Grainger W W Inc-Daily   06/04/99 C=55.625 +1.188 O=54.625 H=55.625 L=54.250 V=2819

10 Day Moving Average

50 Day Moving Average

PRINTED WITH PERMISSION OF OMEGA RESEARCH INC.
Charts created using Omega Super Charts 4.0

How to Detect and Hop Aboard New Legs

GWW shows a picture of the idealized pullback, the stock broke over a flat top base on Tuesday. As you know many breakouts pullback one to two days before resuming their move. GWW is a multiple buy 1-2-3-4, 180 set-up tonight having pulled back 2 days and making a slightly lower low below Thursday's range this morning, before turning around.

Because the pullback occurs within Tuesday's large range breakout, it is also an Extension Level Boomer. Size buyers on the close suggest there is a strong probability for higher prices Monday. Since this is the first pullback after a breakout over a flat top, there is a good likelihood of an extended move to follow so you may want to try to hold on to a piece.

COOPER TRADING INC.
DAILY LEARNING SHEET
13 MAY 1998

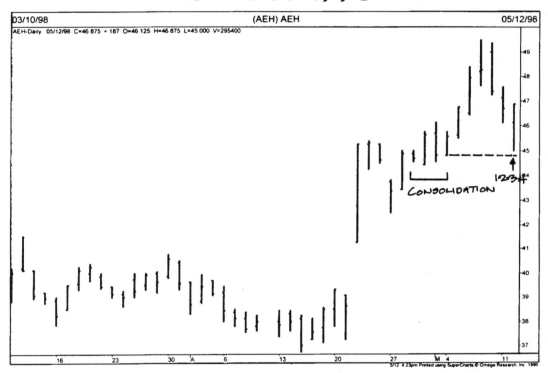

1-2-3-4 With Size To Buy

I'm often asked if all signals are created equal. The answer (of course) is no. AEH provides an interesting example of a good 1-2-3-4 set-up. Notice that today the stock sold off but found support (as it should) at the previous consolidation. It then recovers and closes on its high. This is a sign of eager buyers willing to step up to the plate going into the close. What's also interesting is that there were huge buyers bidding for the stock late in the day. By focusing on stocks that behave well (i.e. find support when they should), close well and have size buyers late in the day you will increase your odds of success.

COOPER TRADING, INC.
DAILY LEARNING SHEET
16 OCTOBER 1997

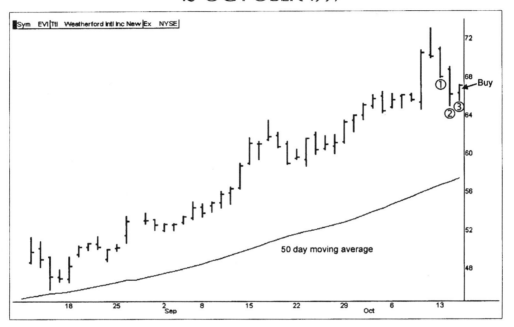

Chart created using Qcharts by Quote.com, Inc.
© 1999 by Quote.com

1-2-3-4 With Size to Buy

EVI, a leader in one of the strongest groups (Oil Service) has a 1-2-3-4 buy set-up for Thursday. Importantly, there was a size buyer on the close and the stock went out on its high.

As you can see, there are other Oil Service stocks with buy signals on both sheets tonight (BJS, CAM, LSS, PDS, RIG) which indicates that institutions are buyers of the group on the pullback. This is a good sign, as much of an individual stock's movement is subject to the action of the group it is in.

COOPER TRADING INC.
DAILY LEARNING SHEET
Tuesday, 29 September 1998

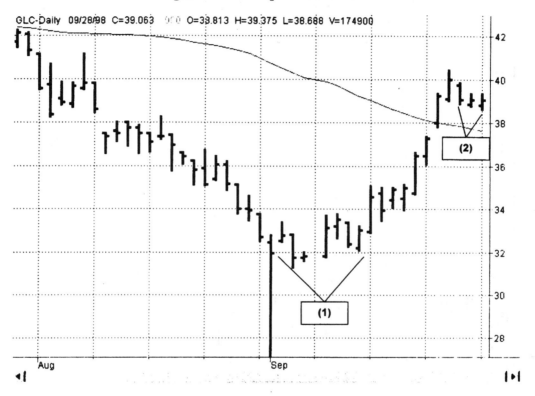

GLC-Daily 09/28/98 C=39.063 O=39.813 H=39.375 L=38.688 V=174900

Shallow Pullback with Substantial Size to Buy

After surging out of a nice bottoming formation (1), GLC has pulled back in a very narrow drift over the last three days (2), leaving us with a 1-2-3-4 buy set-up for Tuesday. The shallow pullback (indicating the stock is in strong hands) as well as the appearance of a steady size buyer(s) throughout the last hour (the stock went out with a <u>substantial</u> bid for 20,000 shares) suggests there is a good likelihood for follow through.

<u>GAP RULE:</u> Any buy recommendation that opens 3/4 point above the stated entry price and any sell recommendation that opens 3/4 point below the stated entry price should be ignored for the day.

Reminder...A signal is not valid unless it trades at or above the entry price for buys and at or below the entry price for short sales

COOPER TRADING INC.
DAILY LEARNING SHEET
23 JULY 1998

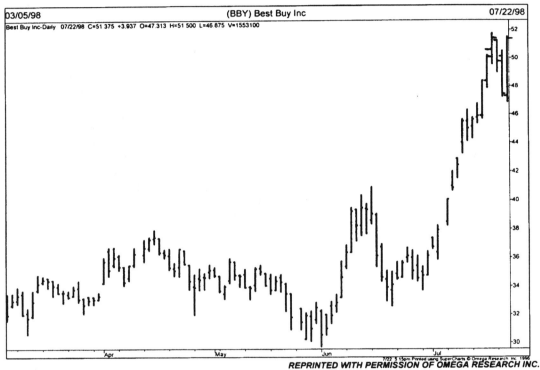

| 03/05/98 | (BBY) Best Buy Inc | 07/22/98 |

Best Buy Inc-Daily 07/22/98 C=51.375 +3.937 O=47.313 H=51.500 L=46.875 V=1553100

REPRINTED WITH PERMISSION OF OMEGA RESEARCH INC.
Chart created using Omega SuperCharts 4.0.

Anticipate 1-2-3-4's

BBY broke out of a two month base in early July to begin a powerful rally. When the stock took out Tuesday's low, it entered the 1-2-3-4 buy position as this was a third lower low. When a strong trending stock gets into a buy position, i.e. the third day or so of pullback, I have found it a rewarding habit to stalk the stock, to watch the behavior. For example, BBY penetrated Tuesday's lows only fractionally at the open Wednesday. However, the stock held its own in spite of a plunging market. For aggressive traders, you can look to go long the 1-2-3-4 position setup and ride these "torpedoes" when the stock takes out the prior day's close (i.e. goes positive on the day). BBY based for three hours around 48 Wednesday and then exploded to 51: the tip-off was the strong intraday relative strength BBY was exhibiting all morning. (See Hit And Run II). Remember, to always keep an eye on the strongest stocks on the Hit List after a few days of pullback; if they're not going down in an ugly market, chances are they're going up. Tonight, BBY leaves us with an outside day 180 and is just shy of being an Expansion Breakout.

COOPER TRADING INC.
DAILY LEARNING SHEET
Monday, 14 December 1998

REPRINTED WITH PERMISSION OF OMEGA RESEARCH INC.
Chart created using Omega SuperCharts 4.0.

Best Buy Inc-Daily   12/11/98 C=49.563 +2.000 O=47.313 H=50.063 L=46.875 V=1641100

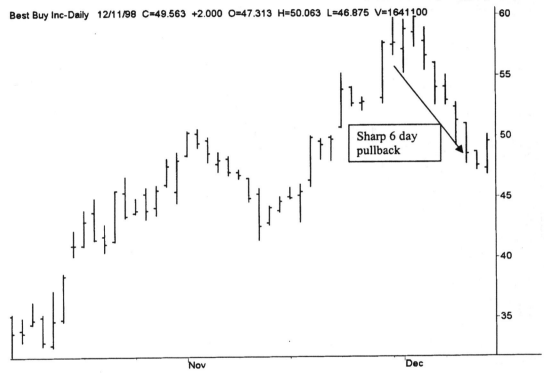

Sharp 6 day pullback

Differentiating Set-Ups – Not All V-Thrusts Are Created Equal

In trying to differential between the many different signals produced by my database every evening, I am looking for something, some kind of inflection in the stock behavior, or something in the pattern that offers me an edge. In the final analysis, often what determines if I'm going to have a profitable day tomorrow – is the ability to separate a good signal from a mediocre signal and a great potential signal from a good signal. What stocks I choose to focus on in my preparation for the following day (as well as my focus and concentration during trading hours) is the cornerstone to successful short-term trading. For example, let's take a look at why I like the V-Thrust set on BBY for Monday.

After breaking out to new all time high in a very strong rally, BBY experienced a sharp 6 day pullback. The fact that the stock traded slightly lower Friday morning but held it's own, reversing to create an outside day, makes the set-up stand out. Moreover, Thursdays narrow range day in spite of a weak market suggested that selling pressure was subsiding; this creates a good likelihood for further follow thru.

COOPER TRADING INC.
DAILY LEARNING SHEET
Tuesday, 15 December 1998

Perkin Elmer Corp-Daily   12/14/98   C=94.438   +2.688   O=91.750   H=94.813   L=91.750

REPRINTED WITH PERMISSION OF OMEGA RESEARCH INC.
Chart created using Omega SuperCharts 4.0.

Strength And Size In A Down Market

As you know, it's important to gauge a stock's performance with the overall market. When a stock rallies when the market is selling off it may be talking. Let's look at PKN. Last week, the stock hits new highs and begins to sell off. Then today, in spite of a very poor overall market, the stock rallies to from a V-Thrusts buy set-up for Tuesday. What makes it even more interesting is that there was size to buy near the close. The fact that these buyer(s) are willing to bid size for a stock in such a poor market suggests that they are anxious to own it. Let's watch this one tomorrow to see if they return.

Gauge a stock's performance with the overall market's. If a stock can rally on a bad day it may be worth a look, especially if there are size buyers near the close.

COOPER TRADING INC.
DAILY LEARNING SHEET
Tuesday, 26 January 1999

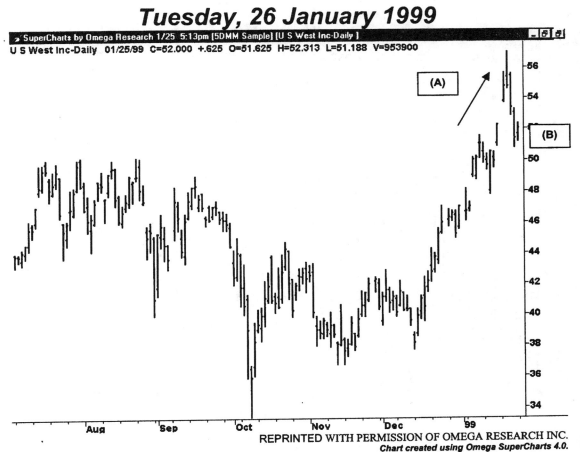

SuperCharts by Omega Research 1/25 5:13pm [5DMM Sample] [U S West Inc-Daily]
U S West Inc-Daily 01/25/99 C=52.000 +.625 O=51.625 H=52.313 L=51.188 V=953900

REPRINTED WITH PERMISSION OF OMEGA RESEARCH INC.
Chart created using Omega SuperCharts 4.0.

1-2-3-4 Pullbacks In A Leading Group

As your know one of the best risk to reward methods for consistently taking money out of the market is to buy strong stocks in a crouch and to short weak stocks when they attempt to stand on their toes. When you select for your pullback candidates those stocks in the very strongest group your edge is enhanced. This is because relentless momentum does not end quickly or easily. Even stocks that <u>have</u> topped typically have a return or reflex rally that tests their highs. This is why the odds are stacked in your favor when you buy pullbacks in the strongest names. When you combine buying the strongest names in the strongest sectors you further improve the likelihood of a winning trade.

Here we have <u>UMG</u>. (In the entertainment and broadcasting group see CCU and CVC). Its quick 1-2-3-4 shakeout back to old highs (A) and Monday's narrow range that closed near the high and above the open suggest UMG is pivoting back in the direction of its strong underlying trend (B).

COOPER TRADING INC.
DAILY LEARNING SHEET
29 JUNE 1998

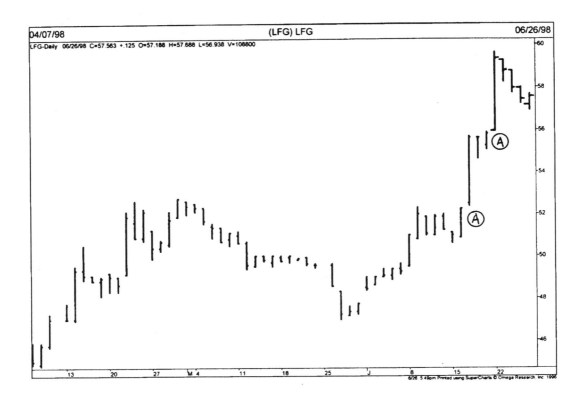

1-2-3-4 + 1

Since most surprises happen in the direction of a trend, one of the best trading edges available, is to identify stocks that have walked off an overbought condition and are poised to snap back in the direction of the underlying impulse. LFG experienced a few large range days recently (A), indicating buying pressure overwhelmed sellers. When a stock contracts on low volume with narrow range pullback days into an expansion or large range day (A), and then closes at the top of its daily range (as LFG did today, Friday), this is often a tip-off that the stock is ready to run again.

COOPER TRADING INC. DAILY LEARNING SHEET 29 MAY 1998

02/13/98   (LHSPF) Lernout & Hauspie Spe CI F   05/28/98

Lernout & Hauspie Spe CI F-Daily 05/28/98 C=53.000 +5.937 O=47.875 H=54.000 L=47.750 V=1997400 Mov Avg 1 line 50.917

REPRINTED WITH PERMISSION OF OMEGA RESEARCH INC.
Chart created using Omega SuperCharts 4.0.

Prior Market Leaders

After a 3 day pullback (which is actually a 1-2-3-4 buy) LHSPF, a prior market leader, finds bottom on 4/27/98 (A). On this same day, the overall market also hits a significant low. The stock then snaps back and tops out on 5/1/98 (B), one day before the Dow hits an all time high. LHSPF then "trades on its own," selling off as the overall market churned sideways. This pullback (C) corrects a longer term up trend. Because the stock has already corrected, it shrugs off this week's sell off and actually closes up slightly (D). Then today, the first up day this week for the overall market, it rallies 6 points to form an Expansion Pivot buy* for Friday. This suggests that LHSPF may once again attempt to regain its position as a market leader.

*Note: Although the set-up looks interesting, use caution due to extreme range.

COOPER TRADING INC.
DAILY LEARNING SHEET
Monday, 15 March 1999

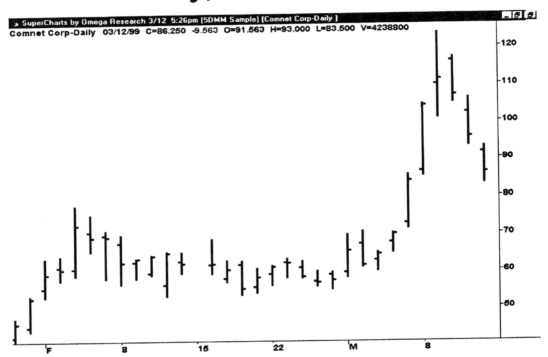

SuperCharts by Omega Research 3/12 5:26pm [5DMM Sample] [Comnet Corp-Daily]
Comnet Corp-Daily 03/12/99 C=86.250 -9.563 O=91.563 H=93.000 L=83.500 V=4238800

REPRINTED WITH PERMISSION OF OMEGA RESEARCH INC.
Chart created using Omega SuperCharts 4.0.

1-2-3-4 Runaway

Tonight, I'm going to show you a twist on my 1-2-3-4 pullback strategy. CNET exploded off a base last week and has pulled back for 3 days. In fact, each pullback day closed near the bottom of the range indicating buyers have backed off in the face of solid profit taking. This is quite normal for a stock that had nearly a 100 % gain in 4 days. Stocks in fast runs typically don't pull back for more than a few days (2 to 4). Since CNET has also pulled back approximately 50 % off the last leg, it provides an interesting set-up. Here is the twist to 1-2-3-4 strategy. Should CNET open below Friday's low and then trade through Friday's low it may indicate a turn. Also, if the stock trades below Friday's low and reverses to go positive on the day, this would be another indication of a rebound. There are few other stocks on our hit list with similar pictures such as VRSN and NTBK. Let's keep an eye on those as well Monday.

Note: CNET is extremely volatile. If this makes you uncomfortable, pass.

COOPER TRADING INC.
DAILY LEARNING SHEET
Monday, 29 March 1999

SuperCharts by Omega Research 3/26 5:58pm [5DMM Sample] [Realnetworks Inc-Da]
Realnetworks Inc-Daily 03/26/99 C=120.000 +1.000 O=115.500 H=120.875 L=114.250 V=6550

REPRINTED WITH PERMISSION OF OMEGA RESEARCH INC.
Chart created using Omega SuperCharts 4.0.

1-2-3-4 Shakeout Pivot

Since breaking out of a 3 month base in January RNWK has been in a powerful uptrend. The first pullback in a strongly trending stock is an odds on bet buy candidate. This is because even assuming that a top is in place- stocks typically have return rallies that test the high.

As you know, trading is more an art than a science. Stocks don't always conform precisely to our strategies and expectations. Often, stocks have more complex pullbacks as opposed to simple 1-2-3-4 pullbacks. Sometimes stocks stutter step before resuming their uptrend in earnest. RNWK had a 1-2-3-4 buy signal on Wednesday night. The stock gapped open coming off Wednesday tail. Friday, RNWK pulled back slightly testing Wednesday's high, but closed at the high of the range suggesting follow thru on Monday.

Many traders won't go back to a situation if it doesn't follow thru picture perfectly. The sign of a superior trader is the ability to reenter on a continuation and/or revalidation of an initial setup-signal. In that vein, if stopped out, remember to reenter RNWK on Monday should the stock retrigger.

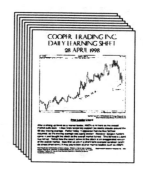

Section III

MULTIPLE SIGNALS

▫▫▫

As I look back over the course of the past several years that I've spent re-fining and applying my trading strategies, I've seen that nothing increases my odds of success within a given trade than when several Hit and Run Strategies are all in agreement with another. In this section we will look at these higher than better odds setups.

COOPER TRADING INC.
DAILY LEARNING SHEET
13 OCTOBER 1997

| 07/16/97 | (EVI) Energy Ventures Inc | 10/10/97 |

Energy Ventures Inc-Daily 10/10/97 C=70^1 -^3 O=70^2 H=73^0 L=70^1 V=650900 Mov Avg 1 line 56^3

50 day moving avg.

Chart created using SuperCharts ™ by Omega Research Inc
REPRINTED WITH PERMISSION OF Omega Research Inc

Expansion Range Double Sticks And A Lizard For Sale

EVI has a Lizard sell set-up for Monday. What's even more intriguing is that the stock gave an Expansion Range Double Stick Signal and had a size seller near the close. I showed the Expansion Range Double Stick Reversal strategy in the Aug. 15 issue of The Hit and Run Trader's Report. It takes into account companies that have a panic-buying day and immediately following a panic-selling day. The selling typically carries over again into the next day. Another piece to the puzzle which underscores the idea of this hysteria to get in and scramble to get out is that the volume on EVI was more than double the norm on both Thursday and Friday.

For new subscribers, I will repeat the Expansion Range Double Stick Rules:
1. Day One (yesterday), a stock must make a 60-day high and its range must be at least the third largest range day of the past 10 days
2. Day Two (today) must close below its opening and its range must be at least the third largest range day over the past 10 days.
3. If rules 1 and 2 are met, we will sell short tomorrow one tick under the day two low and we will risk one point.
4. Use a trailing stop intraday to lock-in profits or exit near close.

The oil sector (to which EVI belongs) is extremely strong, so please remember to use a trailing stop

COOPER TRADING INC.
DAILY LEARNING SHEET
5 FEBRUARY 1998

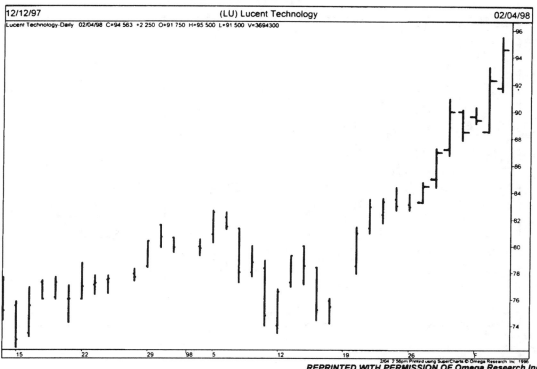

12/12/97   (LU) Lucent Technology   02/04/98

Lucent Technology-Daily 02/04/98 C=94 563 +2 250 O=91 750 H=95 500 L=91 500 V=3694300

REPRINTED WITH PERMISSION OF Omega Research Inc.
Chart created using SuperCharts 4.0.

Focusing On Set-ups With Multiple Signals

In trading, you want as much as an edge as possible. As you know, focusing on set-ups with multiple signals is a good way to create that edge. Wednesday, we had two stocks with multiple signals trigger -- LU and ALL. Both provided solid gains.

There are some other lessons to learn by focusing on Wednesday's behavior in LU. In bull days (strongly trending days in strongly trending stocks), a stock tends to open <u>near</u> its low and close <u>near</u> its high for the day. This is pretty much the case with LU. Also, I have observed that often, if a stock pulls back into the prior day's bar <u>before</u> triggering, this can create a rubberband like effect once the stock triggers. It is often propelled with greater momentum, as many short-term traders are flushed out in the morning pullback creating less overhead supply by this hot money. Keep an eye out for this intraday pattern, it will improve your success.

COOPER TRADING, INC.
DAILY LEARNING SHEET
13 MARCH 1998

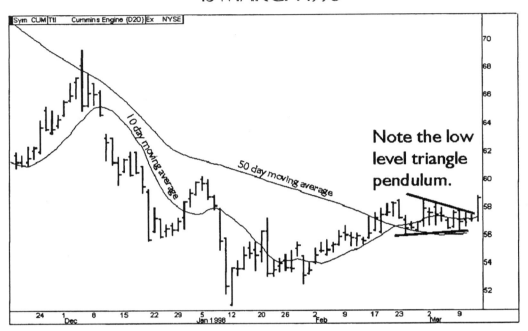

Sym CUM | Ttl   Cummins Engine (D20) | Ex   NYSE

Note the low level triangle pendulum.

10 day moving average

50 day moving average

24 1 8 15 22 29 5 12 20 26 2 9 17 23 2 9
Dec   Jan 1998   Feb   Mar

Chart created using Qcharts by Quote.com, Inc.
© 1999 by Quote.com

<u>Triple Multiple Setup With Size Buyers</u>

CUM (Cummins) has three buy signals for Friday: It is an Expansion Breakout as the stock made a new 60 day high Thursday with a range greater than that of any of the prior 9 days; it is an Expansion Pivot, as the stock is coming off its 50 day moving average; and it also has a 180 buy set-up.

CUM has a nice basing pattern and looks like what I call a Low Level Breakout as well. There appears to be little overhead resistance making this a very good risk-to-reward setup.

To make things more intriguing, CUM had a size buyer(s) at Thursday's close.

COOPER TRADING INC.
DAILY LEARNING SHEET
28 MAY 1998

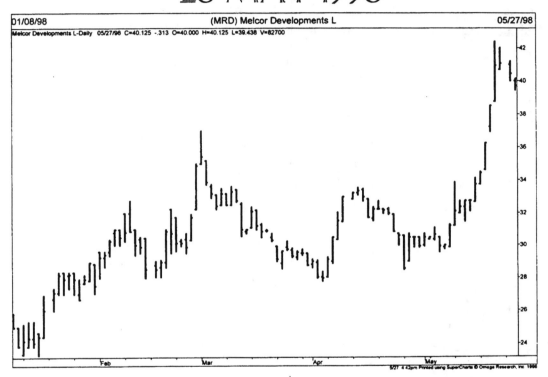

01/08/98   (MRD) Melcor Developments L   05/27/98

Melcor Developments L-Daily 05/27/98 C=40.125 -.313 O=40.000 H=40.125 L=39.438 V=82700

REPRINTED WITH PERMISSION OF OMEGA RESEARCH INC.
Chart created using Omega SuperCharts 4.0.

First Pullback, Multiple Signals With Size

MRD, in the strong chemical group, is a 1-2-3-4/180 buy set-up for Thursday. As you can see from the above chart, despite a market that has seen many stocks experience severe liquidation over recent sessions, MRD has shown persistent strength and undergone only a shallow pullback. This is typically a sign that a stock is in strong hands. Since this is the first pullback after a basing period (during the first 4 months of the year) and adding to the picture the appearance of size buyers on the close, MRD looks like a strong candidate for follow through Thursday.

COOPER TRADING INC.
DAILY LEARNING SHEET
16 JUNE 1998

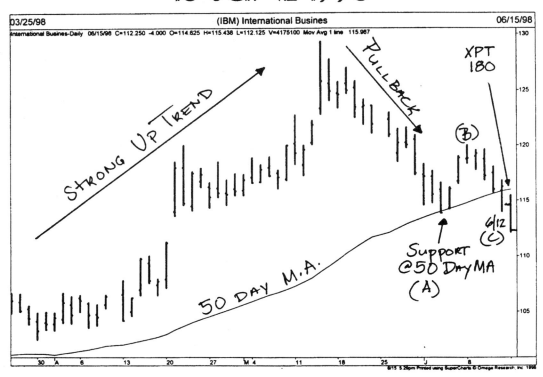

| 03/25/98 | (IBM) International Busines | 06/15/98 |

International Busines-Daily 06/15/98 C=112.250 -4.000 O=114.625 H=115.438 L=112.125 V=4175100 Mov Avg 1 line 115.987

STRONG UP TREND

PULLBACK

XPT 180

50 DAY M.A.

Support @50 Day MA (A)

6/12 (C)

(B)

REPRINTED WITH PERMISSION OF OMEGA RESEARCH INC.
Chart created using Omega SuperCharts 4.0.

Multiple Signals at the 50 Day Moving Average

The 50 day moving average often provides important support and resistance. Why? Because many traders and institutions use it as a benchmark for performance. IBM provides an interesting example. After a strong up trend, IBM pulls back and finds support exactly at its 50 day moving average (A). It then attempts to rally (B) but fails and drops right back to the average. Then on 6/12/98 it stabs below the average but recovers to close just barely above it (C). At this juncture, it still looks potentially bullish as the moving average is tested and the stock held (by closing above the average). However, on Monday, it gaps below the average and proceeds to sell off to form a multiple Expansion Pivot/180 sell signal for Tuesday. This failure at the "50" combined with multiple signals suggests that IBM's up trend may be over.

COOPER TRADING INC.
DAILY LEARNING SHEET
15 JULY 1998

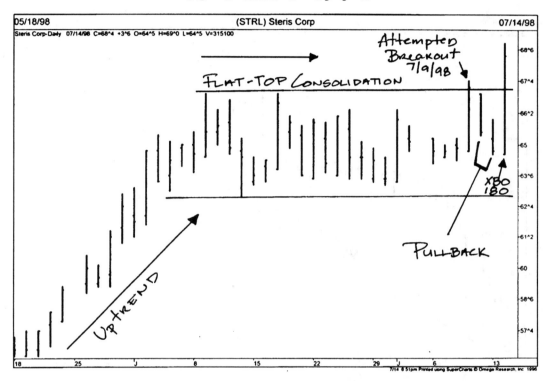

05/18/98   (STRL) Steris Corp   07/14/98

Steris Corp-Daily 07/14/98 C=68^4 +3^6 O=64^5 H=69^0 L=64^5 V=315100

Attempted Breakout 7/9/98

FLAT-TOP CONSOLIDATION

XBO 180

PULLBACK

UPTREND

REPRINTED WITH PERMISSION OF OMEGA RESEARCH INC.
Chart created using Omega SuperCharts 4.0.

Multiple Signals Above A Flat-Top Consolidation

Breakouts above flat-tops can often be powerful. STRL provides an interesting example.
After an up trend, STRL consolidates by going sideways to form a "flat top." Then on 7/9/98, it
attempts to break out, forming an Expansion Breakout buy set-up (shown on fax dated
7/10/98, but didn't trigger) above the consolidation. At this juncture, it looked poised to
explode as the flat top was cleared, it hit a new high and closed at a new closing high.
However, it pulled back into the consolidation for the next two days (still worthy of watching as
stocks very often pullback for 2 to 3 days after a breakout before heading higher). Then today
it decisively breaks out above the consolidation/prior breakout to form a multiple Expansion
Breakout/180 buy set-up for Wednesday. It now appears that all hurdles have been cleared
and STRL is ready to begin its next leg up.

COOPER TRADING INC.
DAILY LEARNING SHEET
9 JUNE 1998

02/11/98	(LFG) LFG	06/08/98

LFG-Daily 06/08/98 C=51.000 +1.750 O=49.500 H=51.000 L=49.500 V=72700 Mov Avg 1 line   48.980

50 DAY MOVING AVERAGE

REPRINTED WITH PERMISSION OF OMEGA RESEARCH INC.
Chart created using Omega SuperCharts 4.0.

Expansion Pivot/180 Buy Set-Up

The bonds have been trending higher lately and are challenging multi-year tops. With this in mind, I thought it would be interesting to take a look at an old friend of ours in the financial sector. LFG has a multiple buy signal for Tuesday. What makes the set-up compelling is that after appearing to undercut a shelf of support ① (apparently setting off stops), the stock has now pivoted above the breakdown point on an expansion of its daily range. ② This action suggests the stock is sold out and that buying is overwhelming selling. Typically, when a stock revisits the scene of the crime (the prior breakdown point) and successfully overcomes what should have been resistance, it is a sign that the stock has renewed the uptrend and is angling for an attack of prior highs.

COOPER TRADING INC.
DAILY LEARNING SHEET
16 JULY 1998

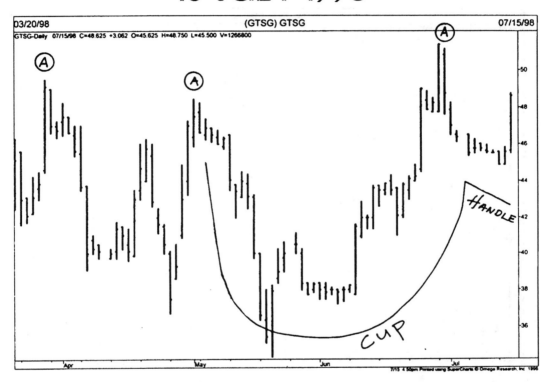

Putting Pieces Together

Let's take a look at a big picture perspective to see how when the short-term dovetails with the larger picture, the ensuing move can be explosive. GTSG (in the strong Telecom group) has built a 7 to 10 week base that has the look of a cup and handle. The stock broke out above double tops two weeks ago and as often happens, pulled back and consolidated in a bullish tight contraction. Wednesday's range expansion in the direction of the underlying trend looks like a pivot off the handle of the larger picture cup and handle.

If GTSG takes out the triple tops in the $50 area (A), it will be a rule of 4 breakout (breakout above triple tops). These are typically dynamic moves. Putting pieces together and having the patience to stalk a stock after an initial thrust will increase your success.

COOPER TRADING INC. DAILY LEARNING SHEET 4 AUGUST 1998

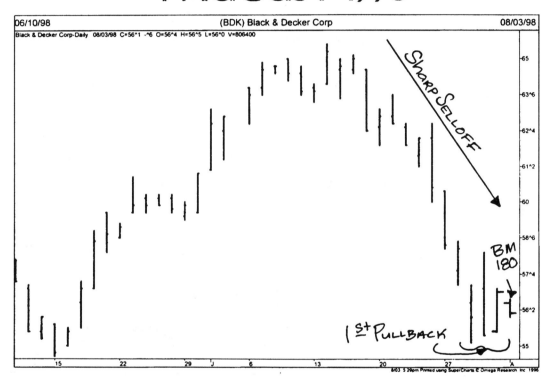

| 06/10/98 | (BDK) Black & Decker Corp | 08/03/98 |

Black & Decker Corp-Daily 08/03/98 C=56^1 -^6 O=56^4 H=56^5 L=56^0 V=806400

REPRINTED WITH PERMISSION OF OMEGA RESEARCH INC.
Chart created using Omega SuperCharts 4.0.

Multiple Signals In The First Pullback

First pullbacks after a breakdown usually provide a good point to enter the trend. When multiple signals occur during that pullback, your odds are even better. BDK provides an interesting example. After hitting all-time highs, BDK sells off sharply. In its first pullback, it forms a Boomer/180 multiple sell short set-up for Tuesday. First pullbacks allow the stock to temporarily walk off an oversold condition. Multiple signals increase your odds as two stand alone methods confirm price action. Should this set-up trigger, the combination of these factors suggest that BDK will resume its downward trend.

COOPER TRADING INC.
DAILY LEARNING SHEET
THURSDAY, 3 SEPTEMBER 1998

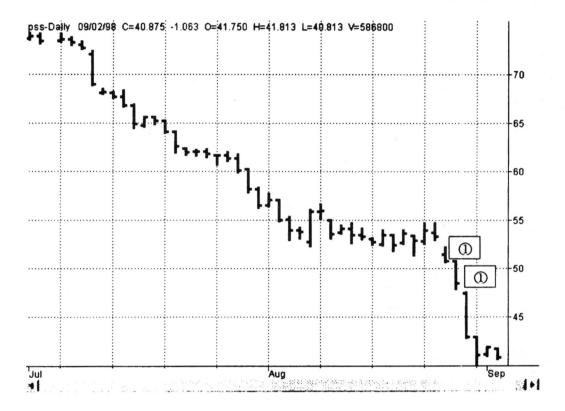

pss-Daily 09/02/98 C=40.875 -1.063 O=41.750 H=41.813 L=40.813 V=586800

Accelerated Moves

Many pieces come together making PSS an interesting short sale for Thursday. As you can see, the stock is in an accelerated downtrend: The Expansion Breakdowns with virtually no pullbacks are indicative of a stock in a <u>fast moving</u> collapse. ①

Even during the market's reflex rally of Tuesday and Wednesday, PSS was unable to bounce, leaving us with a multiple 180/Extended Level Boomer short sale set-up: Apparently there is little institutional sponsorship as sellers line up with stock for sale including an 8,000 share offer on Wednesday's close.

COOPER TRADING INC.
DAILY LEARNING SHEET
Tuesday, 22 September 1998

Caterpillar Inc-Daily 09/21/98 C=42^5 +2^3 O=39^1 H=43^1 L=39^1 V=2041900

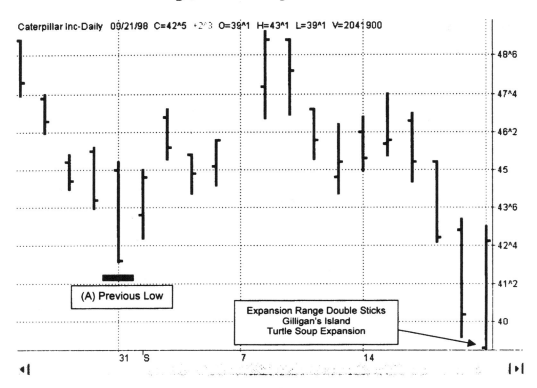

(A) Previous Low

Expansion Range Double Sticks
Gilligan's Island
Turtle Soup Expansion

Triple Signal Reversal

As you know, I would never try to pick a top or bottom of a market. However, reversal patterns such as Lizards and Gilligans are often good for a day trade. Furthermore, Expansion Range Double Sticks and Turtle Soup Expansions can often be good for 2 to 3 days. When you get a combination of these signals, it's even better. CAT provides an interesting example. On Friday, the stock makes a new low. Then today, it makes another new low, but quickly reverses to close above Friday's low and the previous low (A). This forms a multiple Expansion Range Double Sticks, Gilligan, and Turtle Soup Expansion buy for Tuesday. Remember, it's dangerous to be a bottom (or top) picker but when you get multiple signals, the stock may be worth of a look.

GAP RULE: Any buy recommendation that opens 3/4 point above the stated entry price and any sell recommendation that opens 3/4 point below the stated entry price should be ignored for the day.

Reminder...A signal is not valid unless it trades at or above the entry price for buys and at or below the entry price for short sales

Charts created using SuperCharts® by Omega Research, Inc.   Copyright @ 1998, Cooper Trading, Inc.

COOPER TRADING INC.
DAILY LEARNING SHEET
Tuesday, 27 October 1998

United Technologies C-Daily 10/26/98 C=88^1 · O=88^3 H=88^4 L=86^6 V=606300

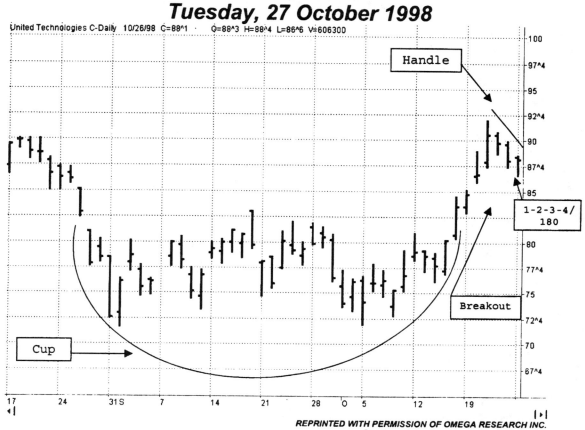

Multiple Signals In The First Pullback

After bottoming for nearly two months, UTX breaks out and rallies sharply. Then in its first pullback, it forms a multiple 1-2-3-4/180 buy set-up for Tuesday. This pullback is significant because it is the first chance the stock has to walk off an extreme overbought condition. In many cases, stocks often continue in the direction of their original thrusts after the first pullback. Also of interest is a bigger picture cup and handle that took several months to form. The combination of the above factors suggests that UTX is poised to challenge its old highs.

By combining multiple signals with first pullbacks and bigger picture analysis, you will stack the odds in your favor.

Section **IV**

MORE PATTERNS
AND STRATEGIES

▪ ▪

Here are a number of setups from favorite patterns that also include Breakouts and Pivots. I have also included some real life examples that I couldn't
categorize but I felt were useful in adding to your trading knowledge.

COOPER TRADING INC.
DAILY LEARNING SHEET
Tuesday, 24 November 1998

Policy Mgmt Sys Corp-Daily   11/23/98   C=49.125   +.562   O=48.563

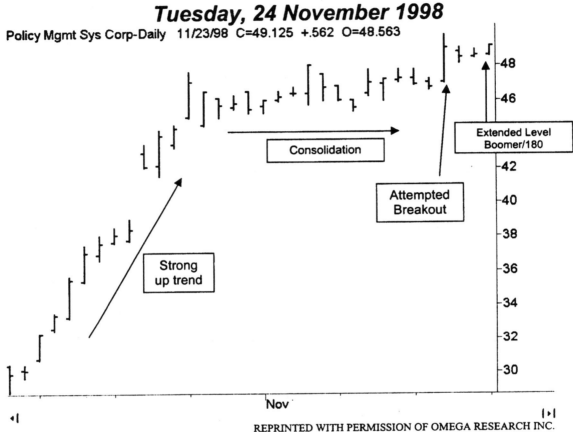

REPRINTED WITH PERMISSION OF OMEGA RESEARCH INC.
Chart created using Omega SuperCharts 4.0.

Choosing Set-ups When The Market Is Up Strongly

When the market is up strongly, the database generates a plethora of buy set-ups. Because many of the stocks are already up strongly (i.e. AMZN up 37 3/8!) it's a good idea to look at less "flashy" set-ups that may have been overlooked by the masses. Stocks that are just coming out of bases, those that have some form of contraction such as Boomers/Extended Level Boomers and 180's at new closing highs often make good candidates. Let's look at PMS. After a strong up trend, it consolidates by going sideways. It then attempts to breakout of the flat top but comes back in and contracts to form an Extended Level Boomer. Then today, it closes up 5/8 to from a 180 buy set-up at a new closing high (and is still an Extended Level Boomer). Because this stock did not make new highs nor was it up some massive amount, it probably was overlooked by the masses. Should the market continue to rally, these "sleepers" often play "catch up" on following days as investors look for potential bargains .

COOPER TRADING INC.
DAILY LEARNING SHEET
19 AUGUST 1998

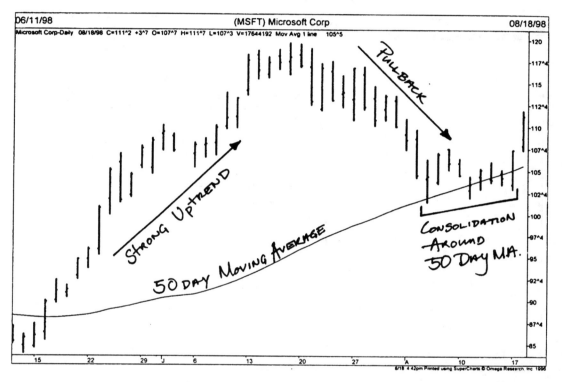

| 06/11/98 | (MSFT) Microsoft Corp | 08/18/98 |

Microsoft Corp-Daily 08/18/98 C=111^2 +3^7 O=107^7 H=111^7 L=107^3 V=17644192 Mov Avg 1 line 105^5

PULLBACK

STRONG UPTREND

50 DAY MOVING AVERAGE

CONSOLIDATION AROUND 50 DAY MA.

Prior Market Leaders/Behavior of Pullbacks

Over the past two days, the market has begun to bounce back from a very oversold condition. I would NEVER try to pick a bottom but often find it profitable to look at prior market leaders when this occurs (remember follow through is key). MSFT provides an interesting example. After hitting new highs, MSFT pulls back in an orderly fashion with the overall market. Then, as if on cue, it stops and consolidates right at its 50 day moving average. Today, it breaks away from the consolidation/moving average to form an Expansion Pivot Buy set-up for Wednesday. The orderly pullback and its behavior around the 50 day moving average suggests that MSFT may once again try to regain its position as a market leader.

COOPER TRADING INC.
DAILY LEARNING SHEET
29 JULY 1998

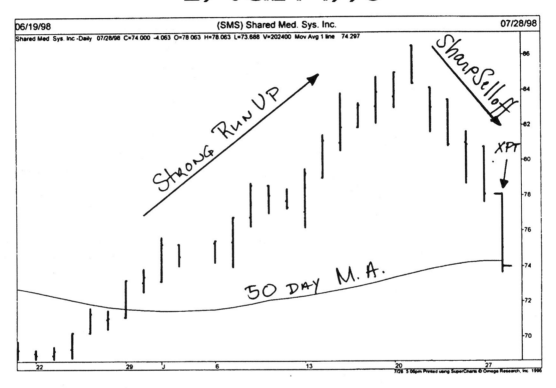

| 06/19/98 | (SMS) Shared Med. Sys. Inc. | 07/28/98 |

Shared Med Sys. Inc -Daily 07/28/98 C=74.000 -4.063 O=78.063 H=78.063 L=73.688 V=202400 Mov Avg 1 line 74.297

REPRINTED WITH PERMISSION OF OMEGA RESEARCH INC.
Chart created using Omega SuperCharts 4.0.

<u>Sharp Angle Expansion Pivot</u>

Many momentum stocks run up and pull back to the 50 day moving average before taking off again. Usually, the pullbacks are in the form of an orderly or gradual sell off. However, when the stock attacks the 50 at a sharp angle, it may be talking. SMS provides an interesting example. After a strong run up, SMS sells off sharply. Then today, it stops just below its 50 day moving average to form an Expansion Pivot sell set-up for Wednesday. Normally, the average provides support as institutions and large investors step up to the plate to support their "darlings" at this critical level. However, when a stock sells off sharply, the downward momentum is often too great for them to stop the carnage. At this juncture, many decide to throw in the towel. Let's stalk this one on Wednesday. Should the Expansion Pivot trigger, the free fall will likely continue.

COOPER TRADING INC.
DAILY LEARNING SHEET
12 JUNE 1998

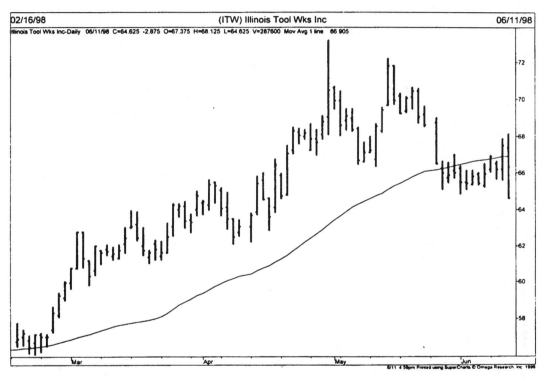

| 02/16/98 | (ITW) Illinois Tool Wks Inc | 06/11/98 |

Illinois Tool Wks Inc-Daily 06/11/98 C=64.625 -2.875 O=67.375 H=68.125 L=64.625 V=287600 Mov Avg 1 line 66.905

REPRINTED WITH PERMISSION OF OMEGA RESEARCH INC.
Chart created using Omega SuperCharts 4.0.

Breakout, Cooked

ITW appeared to breakout of a base, or shelf of support, at it's 50 day moving average on Wednesday. However, on Thursday, the stock reversed sharply completely "offsetting" and eclipsing Wednesday's action, and in the process creating an ouside day Expansion Pivot/180 sell signal. Fakeout Breakouts often lead to fast moves as the hopeful longs scramble to exit.

COOPER TRADING INC.
DAILY LEARNING SHEET
Friday, 18 December 1998

Network Appliance Inc-Daily   12/17/98   C=81.750   +7.625   O=75.000   H=82.125   L=74.250

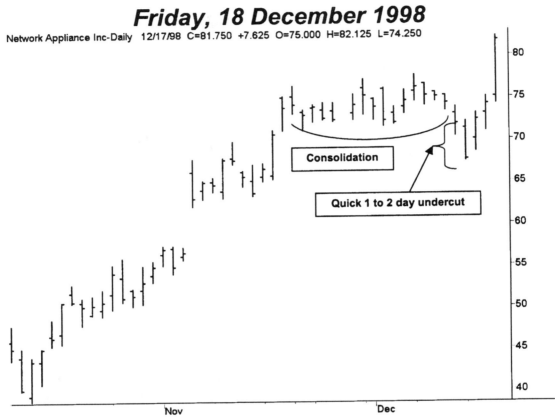

Shakeout Expansion Breakout's

Not all Expansion Breakout's are created equal. A stock that fakes one way and then breaks out the other has a greater likelihood of exploding than a stock that has an "obvious" breakout. This is because stocks that flush out many traders/investors and then turn around are faced with less overhead while at the same time stopped out, sold out bulls must scramble to climb aboard again before the train leaves the station.

As you can see in the above chart, NTAP undercut the three week consolidation, shaking out many players, only to turn around and explode to the upside. This is usually indicative of a new leg.

COOPER TRADING INC.
DAILY LEARNING SHEET
2 FEBRUARY 1998

| 12/01/97 | (BBY) Best Buy Inc | 01/30/98 |

Best Buy Inc-Daily 01/30/98 C=50 625 +2 562 O=48 188 H=50 750 L=48 000 V=593800

Reprinted with permission of Omega Research Inc.
Chart created using SuperCharts 4.0.

Expansion Breakout Continuation Signal

BBY is already in a strong uptrend reflected by a booming ADX reading of 44. (Remember, persistency is the friend of the momentum trader). After a tight sideways consolidation occurring this week, BBY exploded again Friday in spite of a soft stock market (Torpedo). Stocks in fast moves sometimes consolidate their gains by going more or less sideways and pausing for a few days -- you don't always get the pullback in price that comes from short-term profit taking. This is often a sign that the stock is in very strong hands and that demand remains firm.

Let's see if we get a further price expansion Monday on top of Friday's breakout and new high.

COOPER TRADING INC. DAILY LEARNING SHEET 7 MAY 1998

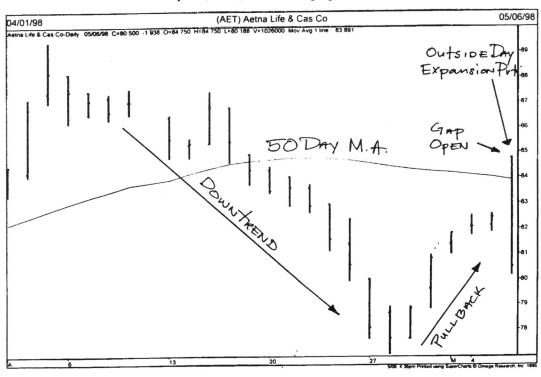

REPRINTED WITH PERMISSION OF OMEGA RESEARCH INC.
Chart created using Omega SuperCharts 4.0.

Outside Day Expansion Pivot

AET provides an interesting Expansion Pivot sell set-up for Thursday. After a strong down trend the stock pulls back. At this point it appears that the downtrend should continue now that the stock has had a "rest." It then gaps open above the 50 day moving average. This attracts longs as the downtrend appears to be over. However, it proceeds to sell off all the way down below the prior day's low forming an outside day. With longs now "trapped" in the stock it should add additional fuel to the sell off should it resume. This could easily bring AET down to recent lows around 77.

COOPER TRADING INC.
DAILY LEARNING SHEET
6 MAY 1998

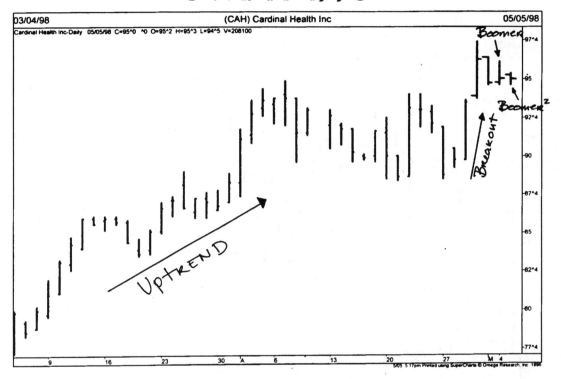

| 03/04/98 | (CAH) Cardinal Health Inc | 05/05/98 |

Cardinal Health Inc-Daily 05/05/98 C=95^0 ^0 O=95^2 H=95^3 L=94^5 V=208100

Boomer Squared

After a breakout, or a strong trend, stocks normally contract or "rest." After this pause, they often once again expand in the direction of the underlying trend. The Boomer set-up was designed to capitalize on this phenomenon. Yesterday, we showed CAH as a Boomer buy set-up. It did not trigger and formed another inside day. A Boomer Squared, if you will. This is further evidence of continued contraction. What makes it even more interesting is the stock paused even though the overall market was down. As you've heard me say before "if it's (a stock in an up trend) not going down, then it's going up."

COOPER TRADING INC. DAILY LEARNING SHEET 22 APRIL 1998

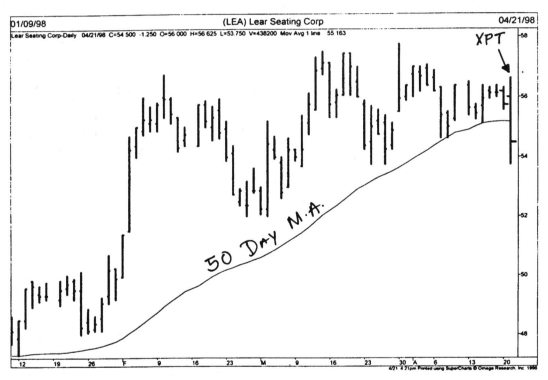

Chart created using Omega SuperCharts 4.0.

Good News Expansion Pivot

In spite of a good day in the stock market and announcing better than expected earnings, LEA was unable to rally today. In fact, the stock sold off to form an Expansion Pivot sell for tomorrow (4/22/98). As technical traders, we often ignore news events. However, when a stock acts in a manner that is totally opposite of the news it often pays to listen. Remember, if it doesn't go up on good news in an up market, then it's going down.

COOPER TRADING INC. DAILY LEARNING SHEET 20 MARCH 1998

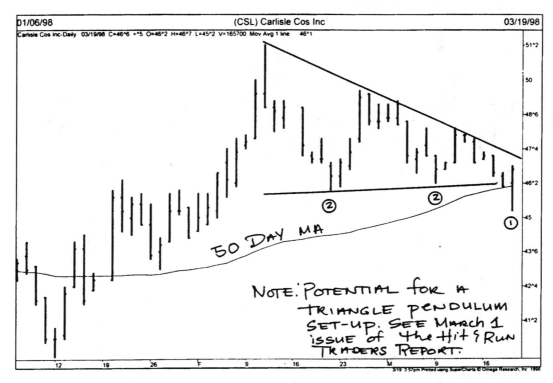

| 01/06/98 | (CSL) Carlisle Cos Inc | 03/19/98 |

Carlisle Cos Inc-Daily 03/19/98 C=46^6 +^5 O=46^2 H=46^7 L=45^2 V=165700 Mov Avg 1 line   46^1

50 DAY MA

NOTE: POTENTIAL FOR A TRIANGLE PENDULUM SET-UP. SEE March 1 issue of the Hit & Run Traders Report.

Expansion Pivot Shakeout

As you know, one of my favorite trading maxims is, " false moves lead to fast moves." The break by CSL below its 50 day moving average on Thursday and subsequent recovery to close on its high has the look of a <u>false</u> breakdown or Fakeout Shakeout. ①

I've observed that often a stock in an uptrend will end a reaction or consolidation on a quick penetration of its 50 day that flushes out the last weak holders. As you can see, interestingly, CSL also broke below prior double bottom support. ② However, what I have found is that more important than the break of support itself is subsequent behavior of a stock.

When a stock breaks support and doesn't follow through and instead reverses to the upside, the stock is speaking -- just as a stock that goes up on bad news (or vice versa) is speaking.

Stocks don't always talk, but listening when they do will improve your success.

COOPER TRADING, INC.
DAILY LEARNING SHEET
30 OCTOBER 1997

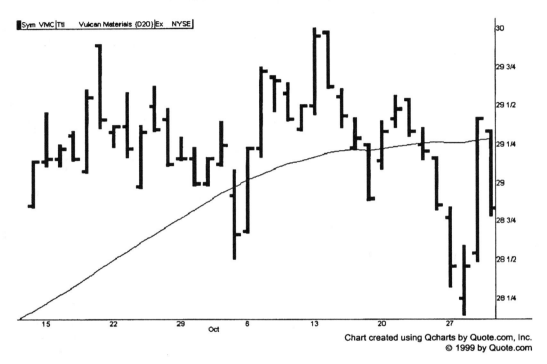

Sym VMC | Ttl   Vulcan Materials (D20) | Ex   NYSE

Chart created using Qcharts by Quote.com, Inc.
© 1999 by Quote.com

VMC (Vulcan Material) has an Expansion Pivot buy signal for Thursday. What makes the set-up interesting is the relative strength VMC has shown during the market decline. Recognizing those stocks with the ability to withstand such market turmoil is a key element in deciding which stocks to stalk.

As you can see, once the market stabilizes and bounces back, these issues can have dynamic moves.

As always, there are no promises, but if VMC follows through tomorrow, an attack of the 30 level looks likely.

COOPER TRADING INC. DAILY LEARNING SHEET 21 NOVEMBER 1997

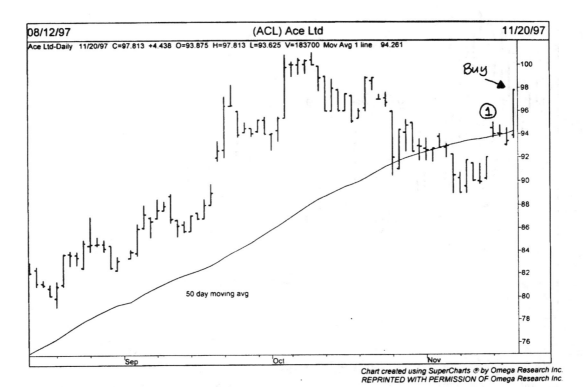

| 08/12/97 | (ACL) Ace Ltd | 11/20/97 |

Ace Ltd-Daily 11/20/97 C=97.813 +4.438 O=93.875 H=97.813 L=93.625 V=183700 Mov Avg 1 line 94.261

Buy

①

50 day moving avg

'Sep   'Oct   'Nov

Chart created using SuperCharts ® by Omega Research Inc.
REPRINTED WITH PERMISSION OF Omega Research Inc.

Multiple Signals In The Direction Of Gaps

ACL (Ace Ltd.) has multiple buy signals (Expansion Pivot and 180) for Friday. What makes this set-up interesting is that ACL, in the strong financial sector, is following through from the gap just above the 50 day moving average on 11/17 ①. That move catapulted ACL above a downtrending resistance line and today's actions appears to confirm the breakout. Add to the picture, a size buyer near the close, and ACL looks poised to challenge its prior high.

Multiple signals that occur shortly after a gap have a better than average likelihood of following through in the direction of that gap.

COOPER TRADING INC.
DAILY LEARNING SHEET 16 JANUARY 1998

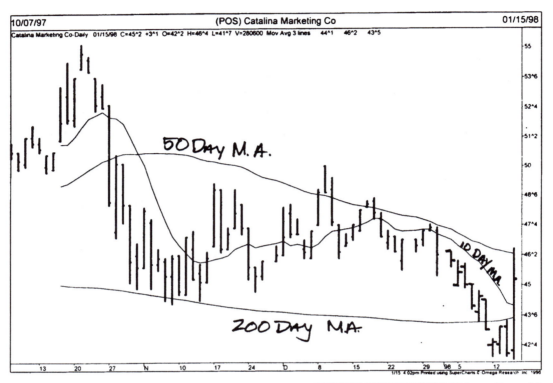

| 10/07/97 | (POS) Catalina Marketing Co | 01/15/98 |

Catalina Marketing Co-Daily 01/15/98 C=45^2 +3^1 O=42^2 H=46^4 L=41^7 V=280600 Mov Avg 3 lines 44^1 46^2 43^5

REPRINTED WITH PERMISSION OF Omega Research Inc.
Chart Created using SuperCharts 4.0.

How to Spot A Possible Intraday Explosion

Let's take a look at the action in POS (Catalina Marketing), a small cap stock that we've traded before.

The stock is in a downtrend, trading below its declining 50 and 10 day moving averages. This morning, POS made a fractional new low at 41 7/8, but never followed through to the downside. At 11:30 am EST, a block of 10,000 shares traded at 41 15/16. At 11:33 am EST, another block of 10,000 shares traded at the same price. Six minutes later another 10,000 share block traded at 41 15/16. This is unusual activity and represents large size for a thin stock such as POS. Did someone know something? Apparently so. At approximately 2:00 pm EST, POS released better than expected earnings and the stock exploded to 45.

When you see this kind of size come in at a new low, it is often a tip-off that the sellers are "cleaned up" and that the stock may turn strongly.

The strategy would be to buy the stock as it turns positive on the day or as it lifts above the price where the size traded, placing a protective stop 1/8 below where the blocks occurred.

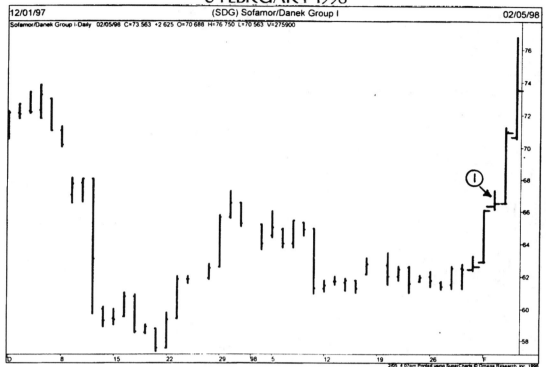

COOPER TRADING INC. DAILY LEARNING SHEET
6 FEBRUARY 1998

REPRINTED WITH PERMISSION OF Omega Research Inc.
Chart created by SuperCharts 4.0.

Pause Days

As I'm sure you realize, trading is a constant learning process. Not only are there new lessons to absorb, but it seems that there are always old ones that need reinforcing. One of the things that I've found to be helpful is to keep a journal of the insights and problems that I've encountered when trading. You'll notice some of the same situations, patterns, and experiences keep repeating. One of the purposes of the Learning Sheet is to bring you in on my own learning process.

One of the things I constantly see happening is that after a signal or breakout by a stock, there occurs what I call a Pause Day. Let's take a look at SDG and you'll see what I mean. On the Learning Sheet dated February 3, I showed the multiple set-up on SDG with a large buyer on the close.

The set-up triggered Tuesday on the open at 66 5/16 and after running up a bit, the stock settled down basically going sideways all day. The stock was digesting the prior days gains during this Pause Day before exploding again. ① Pause Days are typically narrow range days where the stock closes well, i.e. above the open. Often, these days serve to facilitate large buyers prior to a further explosion. As you can see, SDG really did nothing wrong on Tuesday -- it gapped up a little and held that gap on the close. These are some of the inflections in stock behavior to be aware of. I sold half my position on the close Tuesday and was frustrated. However, when SDG revalidated its move on Wednesday, I doubled up on my position.

I will discuss Pause Days more in an upcoming issue of the *Hit and Run Traders Report.*

COOPER TRADING INC.
DAILY LEARNING SHEET
27 FEBRUARY 1998

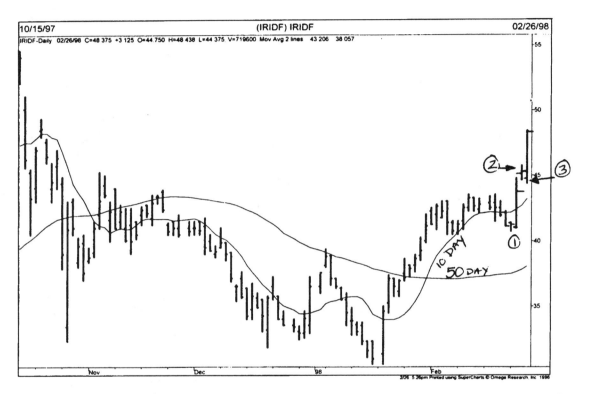

| 10/15/97 | (IRIDF) IRIDF | 02/26/98 |

IRIDF-Daily 02/26/98 C=48.375 +3.125 O=44.750 H=48.438 L=44.375 V=719600 Mov Avg 2 lines 43.206 38.057

. **REPRINTED WITH PERMISSION OF OMEGA RESEARCH INC.**
Chart created using SuperCharts 4.0.

Pause Days Revisited

The Learning Sheet for February 6, 1998, discussed Pause Days and referred to the Pause Day that occurred in SDG (Sofamor Danek) on February 3.

Now let's take a look at IRIDF (Iridium) that had an interesting Expansion Breakout ① set-up over a flat top consolidation (showed on the set-up sheet dated 2/25). Here again, like SDG, the stock triggered the signal with a gap up open (on Wednesday). ② And again, like SDG (on 2/3), IRIDF traded in a narrow range all day basically consolidating Tuesday's gains. After a quick attempt to flush out weak hands on Thursday's open, IRIDF exploded again leaving us with another Expansion Breakout.

Thursday's successful test of the prior day's low ③ was the tip off that IRIDF would attempt a continuation of the breakout. Keep an eye out for this pattern of the morning pullback in a thrusting stock that I call "Ricochet." Adding it to your arsenal of weapons in the battle for profits will improve your success.

COOPER TRADING INC.
DAILY LEARNING SHEET
28 APRIL 1998

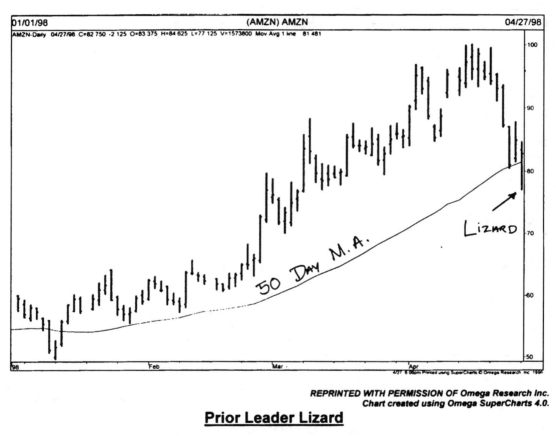

| 01/01/98 | (AMZN) AMZN | 04/27/98 |

AMZN-Daily 04/27/98 C=82 750 -2 125 O=83 375 H=84 625 L=77 125 V=1573800 Mov Avg 1 line 81 481

50 Day M.A.

Lizard

Prior Leader Lizard

After a strong up trend as a market leader, AMZN is hit hard as the overall market pulls back. It then finds temporary support (as stocks should) around the 50 day moving average. Earlier today, it appeared that the free fall had resumed, as the moving average was easily broken. However, bargain hunters came in and bought the stock as the overall market turned. This formed a Lizard buy set-up. Notice how the recent action in this stock is an exaggerated version of the overall market. Now that we are in a short-term oversold condition (and I do stress short-term), it may pay to look at prior market leaders such as AMZN.

COOPER TRADING INC.
DAILY LEARNING SHEET
10 JUNE 1998

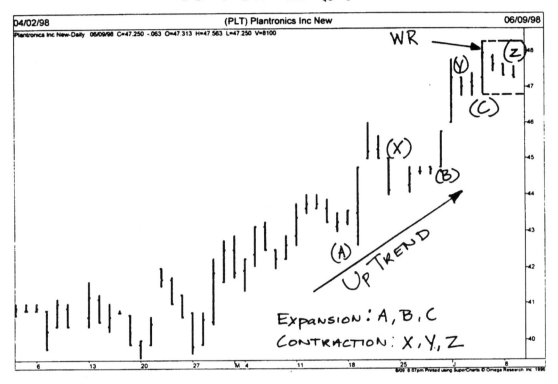

REPRINTED WITH PERMISSION OF OMEGA RESEARCH INC.
Chart created using Omega SuperCharts 4.0.

Expansion/Contraction

Markets tend to move from periods of high volatility (expansion) to periods of low volatility (contraction) and then from low volatility to high volatility and so on and so forth. Like a steel spring, once compressed, it tends to expand. Then, once it has expanded, it tends to compress. Ideally, a stock should expand in the direction of the underlying trend and contract during retracements of that trend. PLT (a 1-2-3-4 buy set-up for Wednesday) provides an interesting example. Notice the expansion at (A), (B), and (C) is in the direction of the underlying up trend and the contraction at (X), (Y), and (Z) is counter to that trend. The latest contraction (Z) consist of 3 days all within last Thursday's (6/4/98) wide range (WR) day (the expansion). This further confirms that PLT has once again contracted. Should this pattern of expansion/contraction continue, PLT could easily challenge its old highs.

COOPER TRADING INC.
DAILY LEARNING SHEET
23 JUNE 1998

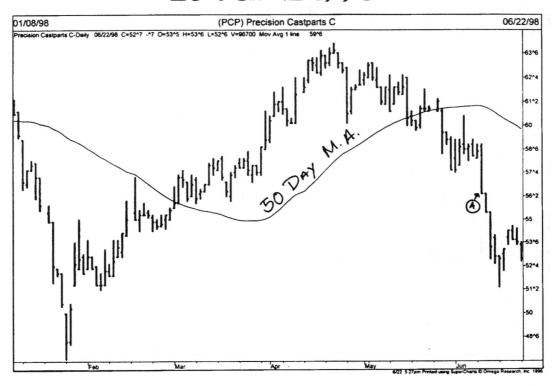

01/08/98   (PCP) Precision Castparts C   06/22/98

Precision Castparts C-Daily   06/22/98 C=52^7 -^7 O=53^5 H=53^6 L=52^6 V=96700 Mov Avg 1 line   59^6

50 Day M. A.

REPRINTED WITH PERMISSION OF OMEGA RESEARCH INC.
Chart created using Omega SuperCharts 4.0.

Snap Back Failure with Size for Sale

After three days of rally, PCP has resumed its strong decline (ADX: 32). The set-up looks interesting because: ① Despite a good tone to the market Monday, PCP faltered. ② The appearance of a size seller(s) near the close and ③ the sharp angle of attack to the downside from June 9th (A) suggests that PCP is undergoing liquidation and may shortly challenge prior lows from early in the year in the 48 vicinity. If you look at a weekly chart of PCP, it is apparent that the stock is in a weak position as the April high was a 2nd lower high. This indicates that the stock has rolled over after a return rally (a rally that tested the highs) and failed.

COOPER TRADING INC.
DAILY LEARNING SHEET
9 JULY 1998

| 04/24/98 | (EGR) Earthgrains Co | 07/08/98 |

Earthgrains Co-Daily 07/08/98 C=57^3 +2^0 O=55^4 H=57^6 L=55^3 V=123300 Mov Avg 1 line   53^6

50 DAY MOVING AVERAGE

How To Spot The Resumption of a Trend

Someone once said the market (and stocks individually) will do the most obvious thing in the most unobvious manner (and frustrate the majority in the process). EGR has been in a strong uptrend (the ADX is still at 30). Yesterday, the stock broke down through an obvious ledge of support (towards the 50 day moving average) but failed to follow through closing nearer to the top than the bottom of the range. (A) When EGR took out the high of Tuesday's breakdown bar, it was signaling higher. Often resumptions of trends will start after these false flushes or shakeouts clear the deck, so to speak (perhaps a seller got cleaned-up). This "boomerang action" -- breaking in one direction only to immediately pivot back strongly in the opposite direction -- typically catapults a stock to a new high.

COOPER TRADING INC. DAILY LEARNING SHEET 12 AUGUST 1998

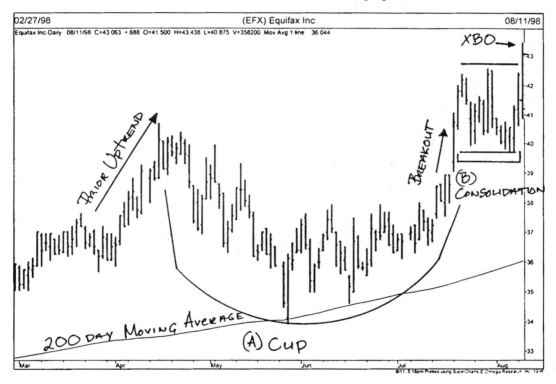

02/27/98   (EFX) Equifax Inc   08/11/98

Equifax Inc-Daily 08/11/98 C=43 063 +.688 O=41 500 H=43 438 L=40 875 V=358200 Mov Avg 1 line 36 044

Combining Short Term Set-Ups With Long Term Patterns

As short term traders, we often only concern ourselves with the last few bars of trading. However, it often pays to consider longer term patterns. EFX provides an interesting example. After a longer term up trend, EFX sells off and stops just above it's 200 day moving average. Over the next two months, it completes a large cup formation. (A) Then after breaking out to new highs, it consolidates for a few weeks by going sideways. (B) Today, it breaks out above the consolidation to close at an all-time high and forms an Expansion Breakout Buy set-up for Wednesday. This in spite of an overall poor market. The stock has now worked off a long-term overbought condition during the cup formation and worked off a short term overbought condition during the recent consolidation. The combination of these bigger picture factors along with a short-term set-up suggests that EFX is now poised to make another leg up.

COOPER TRADING INC.
DAILY LEARNING SHEET
27 AUGUST 1998

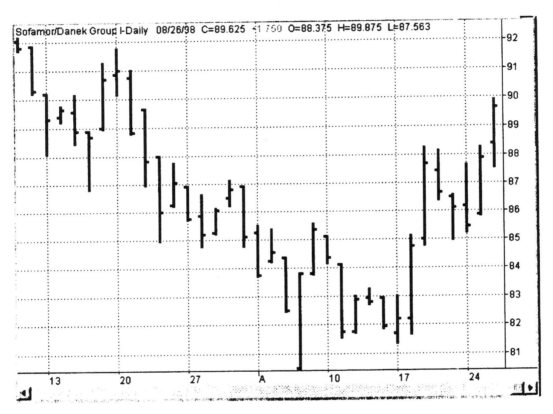

Sofamor/Danek Group I-Daily   08/26/98 C=89.625 +1.750 O=88.375 H=89.875 L=87.563

Small Cap Torpedo

Last night's Learning Sheet shoed the 180 buy set-up on SDG. The glaring disparity between the up open on SDG Wednesday in spite of an ugly open on the market served to focus my attention further.

Once the market stabilized, SDG rallied. This is a good example of the effectiveness of the Intraday Relative Strength Trading strategy. Combining the two pieces, Tuesday's 180 with Wednesday morning's Relative Strength created an edge. Having and edge in trading is often the difference between winning and losing.

COOPER TRADING INC.
DAILY LEARNING SHEET
Wednesday, 23 September 1998

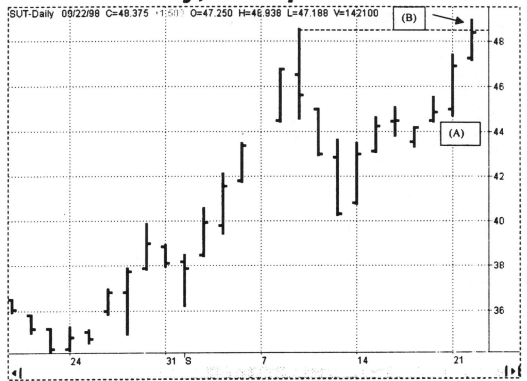

SUT-Daily 09/22/98 C=48.375 +1.500 O=47.250 H=48.938 L=47.188 V=142100

Although SUT is not a set-up for tomorrow, I thought you might find it interesting if I discussed some of the ways I anticipate set-ups. On Monday, SUT was up strongly on a wide range day (A). At this juncture, it appeared that SUT could easily break through the old highs and keep going. Then today, it does make new highs, but fails to break through the prior high with much vigor (B). I term this type of movement "soupy." This means that it has the potential to "cave in" and /or possibly form a Turtle Soup Expansion sell set-up. Also of interest is that a large seller stepped up to the plate near the close. This is exactly the opposite type of behavior you would expect for a stock hitting new highs. Based on the above analysis, SUT is worth watching to get a jump on a potential sell set-up. Just remember that follow through is key. Only take action if the stock continues to show weakness.

<u>GAP RULE:</u> Any buy recommendation that opens 3/4 point above the stated entry price and any sell recommendation that opens 3/4 point below the stated entry price should be ignored for the day.

Reminder...A signal is not valid unless it trades at or above the entry price for buys and at or below the entry price for short sales

COOPER TRADING INC.
DAILY LEARNING SHEET
Monday, 5 October 1998

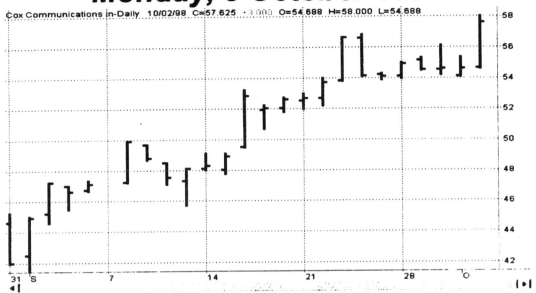

Cox Communications in-Daily 10/02/98 C=57.625 +3.000 O=54.688 H=58.000 L=54.688

Day Over Day Relative Strength

As you know, I am fond of the Intraday Relative Strength Trading Strategy (as explained in Hit and Run II). This is a solid technique for "reading" stocks and catching fast moves intraday. Another similar related strategy that I have used to capitalize on short-term explosive moves in stocks is what I call "Day Over Day Relative Strength." Let's take a look at an example that occurred on Friday. COX (a uptrending name on our Small Cap Hit List) is in a strong uptrend. In spite of the severe market sell Thursday and Friday, COX basically held its ground - staying more or less inside the large range breakout day of 9/23. This is a good indication that the stock is in strong hands. This gives me a reason to stalk the stock as I see the futures rally Friday morning. So, what happens? A size bid appears at the open (5,000 to buy at 54 5/8 at 9:31am). At 9:33am the bid is raised for 5,000 at 55. COX trades up to 56 11/16 within an hour and ultimately trades as high as 58.

This is a great example of the power of putting pieces together: combining the Stepping in Front of Size strategy with the Day Over Day Relative Strength strategy.

GAP RULE: Any buy recommendation that opens 3/4 point above the stated entry price and any sell recommendation that opens 3/4 point below the stated entry price should be ignored for the day.

Reminder...A signal is not valid unless it trades at or above the entry price for buys and at or below the entry price for short sales

COOPER TRADING INC.
DAILY LEARNING SHEET
Wednesday, 7 October 1998

Identifying Which Stocks To Stalk When Using The Intraday Relative Strength Trading Strategy (IRSTS)

I'm sure all of you are familiar with the term Relative Strength and how William O'Neil (IBD) has popularized it to identify the strongest stocks by measuring which stocks are outperforming the majority. The Intraday Relative Strength Trading Strategy (see Hit and Run Trading II) and its cousin The Day Over Day Relative Strength Trading Strategy (see learning sheet for October 5, 1998) are great tools for capitalizing on very short term relative strength outperformance. Let's take a look at two examples that occurred today, Tuesday, and how combining the two strategies captures solid profits.

LXK, which has been a strong stock, and in a return rally to test its highs (9/23) failed on a large range reversal (9/28), suggesting a test failure. Monday the follow through break below its 50 and 10 day moving averages (and the close below both these levels as well as the stocks close below its open) was further confirmation of profit taking and faltering action. Even though LXK "tailed up" on the close on Monday (as the market recovered) the stock remained in a weak position. On Tuesday morning LXK pops open a point and rallies a point further before "Whoopsing" (by taking out Mondays closing price of 65 1/2). This was unusual in as much as LXK was heretofore a strong stock behaving in league with or better than the overall market. However, in spite the futures still being up big, LXK reversed after the first 30 minutes of trading. This was a glaring change in behavior:

1.) LXK was showing poor performance vis-a-vis the S&P futures.
2.) The weak position of the stock as described above was overwhelming the short term positive action in the futures. When the futures came in, LXK buckled, nosediving over 8 points (from its Monday close).

LIT (on our Small Cap uptrending list) was a multiple buy set-up for Monday and triggered providing a quick profit for nimble traders. The stock closed virtually even on the day (Monday) and slightly above its close. LIT held its own Monday and was in a strong position making it a good Day Over Day Relative Strength candidate. Tuesday LIT opened flat and exploded up over 3 points during the markets morning advance.

The tip off – you guessed it – size to buy. 59 5/16 for 5,000 shares appeared at 9:41 EST then at 9:48 EST a 5,000 share bid shows up at 60 1/4. LIT trades up to 62 5/8 quickly.

Intraday Relative Strength Trading and Day Over Day Relative Strength Trading are terrific tools for making money on the long side when the market is weak, and for profiting on the short side when the market is strong. Both strategies do a great job of creating profits by gauging and then exploiting a stocks behavior against the overall market.

GAP RULE: Any buy recommendation that opens 3/4 point above the stated entry price and any sell recommendation that opens 3/4 point below the stated entry price should be ignored for the day.
Reminder...A signal is not valid unless it trades at or above the entry price for buys and at or below the entry price for short sales
Charts created using SuperCharts® by Omega Research, Inc.   *Copyright @ 1998, Cooper Trading, Inc.*
Past results are not indicative of future returns. There is a high degree of risk in trading. Cooper Trading Inc. assumes no responsibility for your trading results. Principals of Cooper Trading Inc. may at times maintain directly or indirectly positions mentioned in this service.

COOPER TRADING INC.
DAILY LEARNING SHEET
Monday, 26 October 1998

Symbol Technologies I-Daily 10/23/98 C=45^1 -4^1 O=48^7 H=49^0 L=44^1 V=639800 Mov Avg 1 line   46^0

(A)

50 Day Moving Average

Aug   Sep   Oct

When Stocks Don't Act As They Should

After the bell on Thursday, SBL (on our Hit List) released earnings that were better than expected. However, the stock opened down Friday, and substantial size for sale (26,500 shares at 47 3/4) showed up at 10:13am EST. When there is good news and a stock doesn't act as it should and you see size for sale there is a good likelihood that the stock will trade lower. Why? Often it means everyone who was interested in buying was loaded up and/or expectations for an earnings surprise were even greater than the reality. Bottom line, too many traders/investors were leaning to one side of the boat. When this occurs in the area of a prior breakdown level (as is the case with SBL – note the breakdown of the stock on 10/01 **(A)** where sellers swamped buyers – often stocks return to the "scene of the crime" and kiss the resistance one last time) a stock is often very vulnerable. SBL leaves us with a multiple sell signal, a 180/Expansion Pivot. Due to SBL's large range on Friday, should the stock pop open on Monday you may want to consider using the Whoops Strategy for a more aggressive, earlier entry. (Remember the Whoops Strategy triggers when a stock pops open and takes out the prior days <u>close</u>.)

COOPER TRADING INC.
DAILY LEARNING SHEET
Friday, 30 October 1998

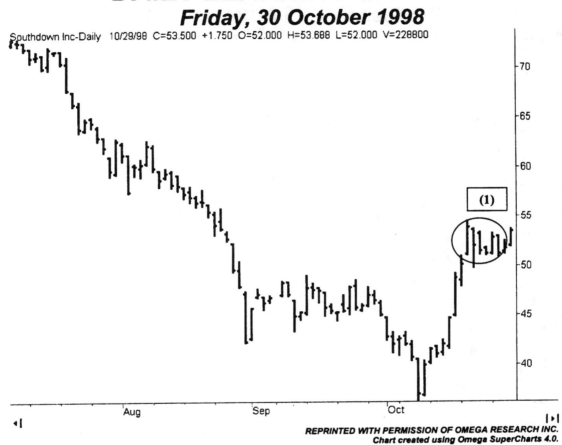

Southdown Inc-Daily 10/29/98 C=53.500 +1.750 O=52.000 H=53.688 L=52.000 V=228800

REPRINTED WITH PERMISSION OF OMEGA RESEARCH INC.
Chart created using Omega SuperCharts 4.0.

Breaking Out With Size To Buy

Sometimes stocks walk off a short-term overbought condition by consolidating sideways rather than pulling back. This occurance is usually quite bullish when the consolidation takes the shape of an orderly drift contained or "wedged" within the high area of the up thrust. The pattern is typically referred to as a pennant **(1)**. Because SDW closed near its low Wednesday in a narrow range day yet pivoted back strongly on Thursday closing on its high,(with size to buy at the bell) the stock appears coiled and poised to follow through on its breakout from the pennant. As you can see, should SDW follow through, there is no overhead resistance until perhaps the $ 60 area. This creates a solid risk to reward set-up.

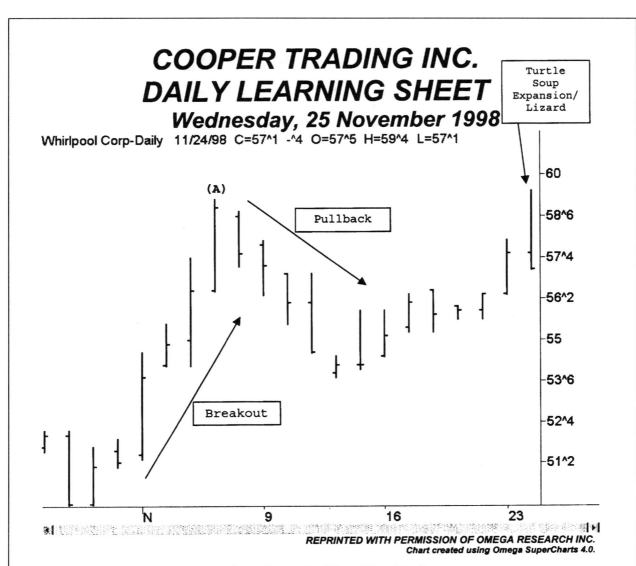

COOPER TRADING INC.
DAILY LEARNING SHEET
Wednesday, 25 November 1998

Turtle Soup Expansion/ Lizard

Whirlpool Corp-Daily 11/24/98 C=57^1 -^4 O=57^5 H=59^4 L=57^1

(A)

Pullback

Breakout

REPRINTED WITH PERMISSION OF OMEGA RESEARCH INC.
Chart created using Omega SuperCharts 4.0.

Turtle Soup Expansion/Lizard Combination

The Turtle Soup Expansion pattern was designed to identify potentially false breakouts. When combined with bigger picture analysis and other reversal patterns such as the Lizard it gives us additional clues that the breakout has failed. Let's look at the WHR. After breaking out, WHR pulls back and then resumes its up trend. So far, the stock is acting as it should. However, today it hits new highs but caves in and closes on its low to form a multiple Turtle Soup Expansion/Lizard sell combination for Wednesday. The new highs attracted the breakout players as the "Johnny come lately's" dog piled into the stock. The fact the stock "tailed" and caved in on a wide range suggests that a short term panic was caused as these players scrambled to exit the market. In addition, those that bought the previous peak(A) and were looking to "get out even" are probably now frustrated because they missed their opportunity. The combination of the above factors suggests that WHR still has some unfilled sellers.

COOPER TRADING INC.
DAILY LEARNING SHEET
Thursday, 7 January 1999

Novellus Systems Inc-Daily 01/06/99 C=66^1 +7^4 O=59^7 H=67^6 L=59^7 V=4724400

When To Hold'em

On the fax for Tuesday (dated 1/5/98), I showed a stand alone buy signal for Novellus (NVLS) in the semi-conductor equipment maker group. The set-up triggered at 53 and the stock closed at 58 9/16 near the top of its range for the day. There are multiple reasons why the position (or at least a piece) should have been held overnight.

1) Tuesday's action created another signal, an Expansion Breakout. Signals on top of signals (piggyback signals) typically lead to further gains.
2) As mentioned before, NVLS closed near the top of its range, an additional reason for carrying over the position.
3) The stock made a new high as well as a <u>new closing high.</u> Stocks making new closing highs, particularly on an expansion in range, usually continue their momentum.
4) I don't usually discuss head and shoulders patterns, but they are popular. As you can see, NVLS broke above a potential right shoulder on Tuesday. (A) Wednesday's upside move demonstrates what happens with failed patterns. They can be explosive. When the players who were convinced of a potential head and shoulders top in the making were proved wrong, the stock spoke loudly. I hope you all took a piece out of this move.

COOPER TRADING INC.
DAILY LEARNING SHEET
Tuesday, 19 January 1999

Plantronics Inc-Daily 01/15/99 C=81.250 +.250 O=80.625 H=81.250 L=80.000 V=596

REPRINTED WITH PERMISSION OF OMEGA RESEARCH INC.
Chart created using Omega SuperCharts 4.0.

Expansion, Contraction

One of the most consistent methods for taking money out of the markets is buying pullbacks on strongly trending stocks. The nature of fast moving stocks is to (1) thrust, (2) pause or pullback, and (3) pivot back in the direction of their powerful underlying trend. The pause or pullback can take the form of a more or less sideways consolidation in time or a quick pullback in price. Both allow the stock to walk off a short-term overbought condition. Often a stock will tip its hand as to when it's ready to resume its trend by a contraction in range over a day or two. This typically indicates a balance point – suggesting short term selling pressure/profit taking has subsided.

One of my favorite set-ups is to find a thin stock in this position that has basically stayed even on the day when the market has exploded (as large players seek to accumulate positions in a smart fashion without alerting the trading world). These stocks often play catch up in a big way during the subsequent session. PLT, Plantronics, is a good example. The stock has pulled back into its strong impulse (A) and has contracted (B). PLT looks wound up and poised to spring in an attack on prior highs. Keep in mind stocks have cycles of contraction and expansion. Thinking in these terms will give you an edge.

COOPER TRADING INC.
DAILY LEARNING SHEET
Tuesday, 16 February 1999

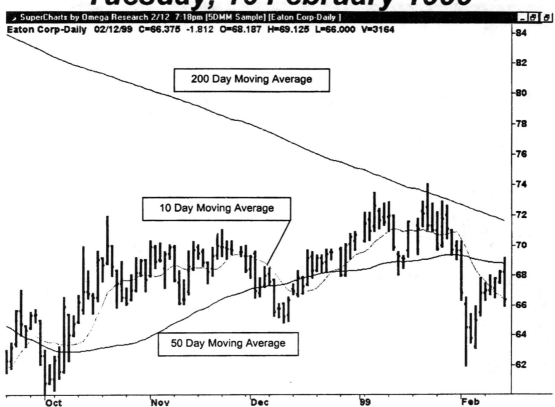

SuperCharts by Omega Research 2/12 7:18pm [5DMM Sample] [Eaton Corp-Daily]

Eaton Corp-Daily 02/12/99 C=66.375 -1.812 O=68.187 H=69.125 L=66.000 V=3164

200 Day Moving Average

10 Day Moving Average

50 Day Moving Average

REPRINTED WITH PERMISSION OF OMEGA RESEARCH INC.
Chart created using Omega SuperCharts 4.0.

Pullback Shorts

Tonight's example is short and sweet. ETN is a laggard as the stock could not even break above its declining 200 day moving average in the market's strong rally off the October lows. Friday's outside day/ 180 at the 50 day resistance leaves the stock vulnerable. The picture shows how a stock often walks off an oversold condition by pulling back to kiss the breakdown area goodbye before once again resuming the bias towards new lows.

COOPER TRADING INC.
DAILY LEARNING SHEET
Tuesday, 9 March 1999

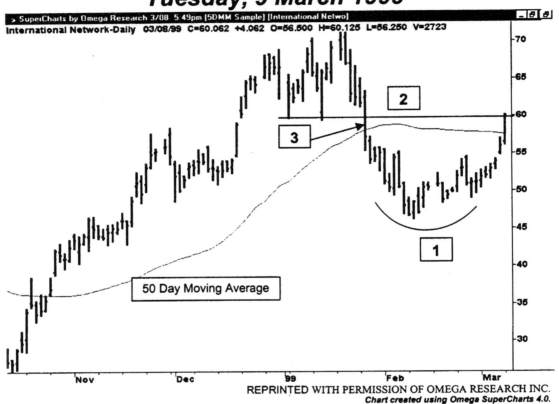

> SuperCharts by Omega Research 3/08 5:49pm [5DMM Sample] [International Netwo]
International Network-Daily 03/08/99 C=60.062 +4.062 O=56.500 H=60.125 L=56.250 V=2723

50 Day Moving Average

REPRINTED WITH PERMISSION OF OMEGA RESEARCH INC.
Chart created using Omega SuperCharts 4.0.

Wearing Two Hats

Capturing stocks as they reassert their primary trend, after an intermediate correction, often creates a good opportunity to take money out of the market.

INSS formed a relatively tight saucer bottom **(1)** after flushing out longs when the stock nose-dived through its 50 day moving average. Often when stocks cross back above the 50 day moving average they are ready to challenge their prior highs. As you know many times prior bases become resistance, (and similarly prior resistance acts as support). If INSS penetrates the prior breakdown point at $60+ **(2)** (the prior base) it appears the stock will be reasserting the uptrend. It will be a sign of strength if INSS "offsets" the breakdown day, (1/26).**(3)**

Should the test fail, and market dynamics turn unfavorable Tuesday, INSS may then present a shorting opportunity. Never be a dyed in the wool bull or bear – be ready to turn with the tide - let the market be your Guru. Listening to stocks speak requires flexibility. Don't be married to preconceptions.

COOPER TRADING INC.
DAILY LEARNING SHEET
Tuesday, 13 April 1999

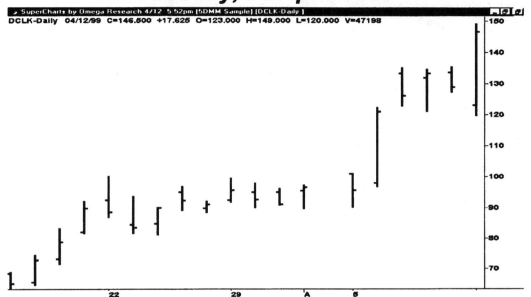

♪ SuperCharts by Omega Research 4/12 5:52pm [5DMM Sample] [DCLK-Daily]
DCLK-Daily 04/12/99 C=146.500 +17.625 O=123.000 H=149.000 L=120.000 V=47198

PRINTED WITH PERMISSION OF OMEGA RESEARCH INC.
Charts created using Omega Super Charts 4.0.

Anticipating 180's and Reversals with Specialist Delight Openings

When the market makers and specialists have time on their side (as in overnight and particularly over a weekend) to prepare for news-- good or bad-- you have to think in terms of trading along with them- not against them. Hey, specialists aren't there to be taken. Such was the case this weekend with the S&P futures down as much as 30 points on Compaq's post bell Friday warning.

What often occurs in the case of bad news in a market up-trend is the specialists/market makers will pull the plug-- opening stocks close enough and low enough to where they might be interested (or where they "know" institutions will step-up). If you're already long and wrong on the open- you've already taken the heat. Why not see if the inevitable bounce can mount a head of steam and turn the tide.

The best names to anticipate for reversals are stocks in runaway trends that are no more than 1 to 3 days off their highs and that closed at/near their lows. That's critical. Why? The pullback indicates profit taking; the low close suggests hot money and short term traders are probably out and not carrying over the stock- particularly in front of a weekend. This creates less overhead supply- short term and therefore ease of movement higher.

The gap down day (or early trade down to below the prior day's low) sets up the potential for a reversal day. Once the stock A) takes out its morning range, and B) the prior day's low and C) goes positive on the day the die is cast for a reversal day. Going positive after the hook down opening often inspires explosive moves as wrong-footed traders scramble to re-asses their preconceptions. Tonight we have two examples of such trades on our sheet; DCLK and AWRE whose multiple signals suggest continuation suggest moves for Tuesday.

Section V

STOPS AND PROFIT TAKING

● ●

As I stated in the introduction, stops and profit-taking are the most important aspect of trading. Every successful trader I know is vigilant about using tight stops and minimizing their losses. This, more than any other aspect of trading, will be the difference between whether you succeed or fail.

COOPER TRADING, INC.
DAILY LEARNING SHEET
29 OCTOBER 1997

Chart created using Qcharts by Quote.com, Inc.
© 1999 by Quote.com

<u>Trading Defensively and Pro-actively</u>

On Monday I decided it would be in everyone's best interest not to trade the Hit and Run Set-ups on Tuesday. Why? Because the sell-off left us with hundreds of Expansion Breakdown sell signals and Expansion Pivot sell signals, yet we closed in grossly oversold conditions. The set-ups told me the market would certainly sell off in the morning (and triggering our short sales) but the oversold condition told me there was a high likelihood of a major intraday reversal. The smartest and the most defensive move was to ignore the set-ups and act defensively.

Please remember; this is a momentum-based methodology that I use and when the momentum moves to an extreme, we must acknowledge it and pass on the set-ups (as I did Tuesday). Also, we had very large gains on the short side on Monday and it makes no sense to risk your profits when the volatility is at extreme levels.

Because trading is an everyday profession, it allows us to be patient and trade when the odds are in our favor.

COOPER TRADING, INC.
DAILY LEARNING SHEET
05 NOVEMBER 1997

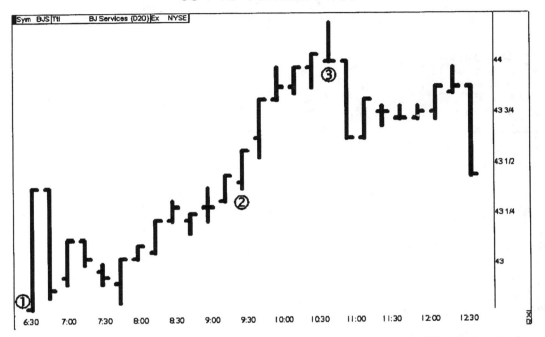

Chart created using Qcharts by Quote.com, Inc.
© 1999 by Quote.com

Locking in Profits

Tonight's sheet is a reminder on locking in intra-day profits. Today, ① we bought BJS at 86 1/8. When there is a 1 point profit, ② you should move your stop to break-even (your entry) and consider taking profits on half. When the profit rises to 2 points, ③ you should definitely sell at least ½ your position and move your stop on the other half to 1 point profit in case the market reverses.

Exit strategies are move difficult than entry strategies, but with practice it becomes second nature.

COOPER TRADING INC.
DAILY LEARNING SHEET
6 JANUARY 1998

Equity **IGPO**

Screen printed.

2-DAY CHART   FNM US $ 14:3

INTERVAL SIZE (MINUTES) ▮▮   VOLUME (Y/N) ▮
MOV AVG PERIODS ▮▮ ▮▮   BAR/CANDLE CHART? (B/C) ▮   VOL MOV AVG PERIODS ▮▮ **N**
HI 59⁵⁄₈ N Lo 57¹⁄₈ N Vol 2284200 13:01 ↑   **58¹⁄₈**   −¹⁄₁₆

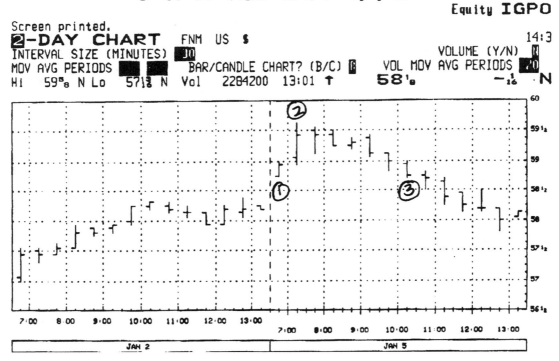

Scratching A Trade

Let's look at the importance of using trailing stops. ①Today, we had an Expansion Breakout trigger at 58 3/4 and our original protective stop was at 57 1/2. ②When the stock rose as much as 1 1/16 points higher, you should strongly consider taking profits on a piece, but more importantly, you need to move your protective stop up to break-even. ③This allows you to scratch the trade (on a worst case scenario) and preserve your capital.

This lesson took me years to learn, but I believe it is what makes the difference between a winning trader and a losing trader.

COOPER TRADING INC.
DAILY LEARNING SHEET 8 JANUARY 1998

1-DAY CHART   TKC US $ 14:1
INTERVAL SIZE (MINUTES) **20**   VOLUME (Y/N) N
MOV AVG PERIODS ▮ ▮   BAR/CANDLE CHART? (B/C) **B**   VOL MOV AVG PERIODS **50**
HI   82⅝ N Lo   80 N Vol   157100 13:01 ↓   **81⅛**   +1⅛   N

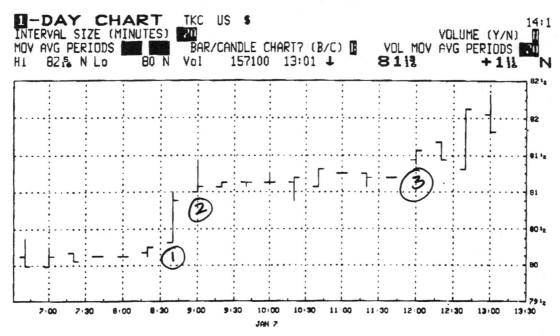

REPRINTED WITH PERMISSION OF BLOOMBERG L.P.

Maximizing the Small Cap Service and Adding To A Position

One of the ways to optimize the Small Cap service is to pay close attention to the possible Stepping In Front Of Size carryover section at the bottom of the daily fax. When a signal exists combined with size buyers (or sellers in the case of short set-ups) near the close, there is a good likelihood of follow through as these buyers haven't been able to get filled.

The Lizard buy set-up on TKC, with a size buyer at the close, on Wednesday's sheet, is a good example of what I'm referring to. The size buyer and seller feature of the Small Cap service gives us an edge: use it to your advantage.

One of the questions I'm asked frequently concerns adding to a position. The above intraday chart on TKC illustrates when and why I added to my position today.

> 1) The Lizard signal is triggered at 80 1/4 and a size bid shows up at 80 1/4, a good sign.

> 2) In spite of an ugly market, a bid for 5,000 shares comes in at 81 and is quickly increased to 10,000 shares. I add to my position.

> 3) The overall market begins to reverse and a size bid for 5,000 shares shows up at 81 1/4. It is immediately raised to 81 3/8, and I add to my position again.

Since TKC closed strongly in our favor, at least a piece should have been carried over.

COOPER TRADING INC.
DAILY LEARNING SHEET
12 JANUARY 1998

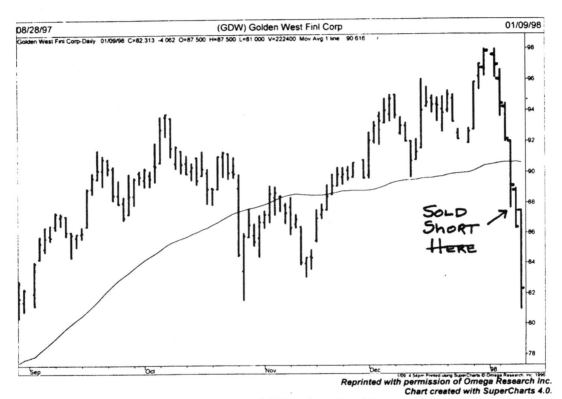

| 08/28/97 | (GDW) Golden West Finl Corp | 01/09/98 |

Golden West Finl Corp-Daily 01/09/98 C=82.313 -4 062 O=87 500 H=87 500 L=81 000 V=222400 Mov Avg 1 line 90 616

Reprinted with permission of Omega Research Inc.
Chart created with SuperCharts 4.0.

How to Milk A Winning Position

On the sheet dated January 8 (for Thursday), we had an Expansion Pivot short signal on GDW. The set-up triggered at 87 5/8 and since the stock closed strongly in our favor (86 3/8, at the low of the day) a piece should have been carried over. On Friday, GDW popped up 1 1/8 on the open to 87 1/2. Ordinarily, I would be covering a position that retraced that much. However, since the rebound occurred on 1 tick, the opening, I have found it a better policy to put my stop just above the morning range (say 1/4 to 3/8 of a point above) and make the stock "prove itself."

I say this because I am aware that often (not always) the opening print of a stock in a strong downtrend or fast break is "engineered." Call me a cynic, but many times it appears either a market maker has been inundated with sell orders near the prior day's close and "requires some relief" or perhaps a fund is trying to "protect" a position (See the Whoops chapter in Hit and Run Trading). Maybe a nervous short just wants to cover based on the opening S&P action or because of the latest economic report. Either way, if the stock can't follow through from the open, the likelihood is that any sponsorship is thin to nil.

A little patience can pay big dividends: GDW collapsed on Friday trading as low as 81!

COOPER TRADING INC.
DAILY LEARNING SHEET 16 MARCH 1998

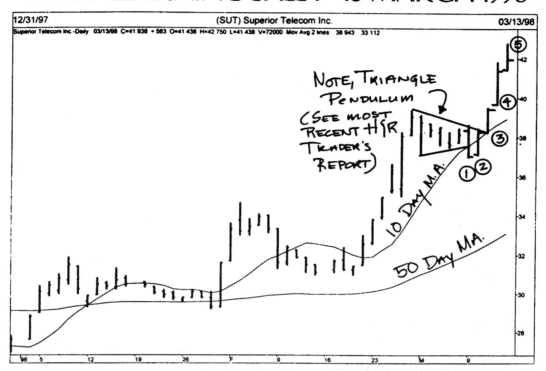

Reprinted with permission of Omega Research Inc.
Chart created using SuperCharts 4.0.

The Difference Between Winning & Losing

Let's step back and take a look at our set-ups and trades on a stock on our Hit List this past week.

SUT (ADX 42) was shown as an HG2 buy on the sheet dated 3/9. ① The signal triggered early on Monday's session, but never really got going (a good candidate to scratch) ultimately stopping us out. However, the next day, 3/10, SUT sprang back strongly creating a 180 buy set-up for us (shown on the fax dated 3/11). ②

Now, the most natural reaction among many would be, "No way -- I'm not taking this set-up, I just lost money on this one the other day." You know...once bitten, twice shy. However, I've found that one of the biggest mistakes traders make, myself included, is not going back to a situation a second or third time if the stock revalidates itself.

As a trader I admire once said, "Markets can spin on a dime and most traders cannot." To win at this game, you have to stay focused (that's the purpose of the Hit List) and stay flexible.

SUT proves the point. The 180 set-up triggered at 38 1/2 on Wednesday (3/11) ③ and SUT closed on its high (39 1/2), a new all-time high. We hold. Thursday morning the stock gaps open slightly and explodes for another 2 points -- are we having fun yet? ④ Friday, SUT followed through for another point and change and our tight trailing stop was hit as SUT succumbed to some mild profit taking. ⑤ The moral of the story: The more focused and flexible you are, the more successful you will be.

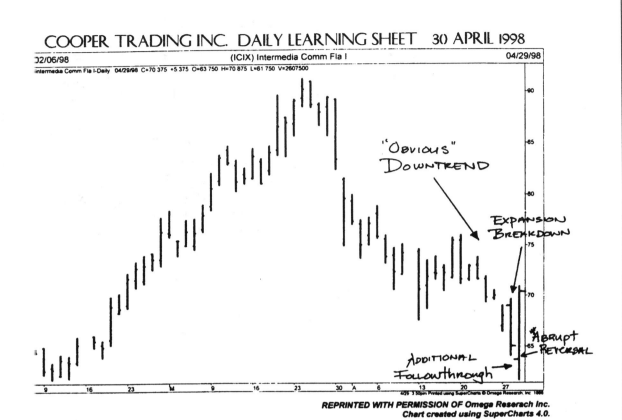

COOPER TRADING INC. DAILY LEARNING SHEET   30 APRIL 1998

02/06/98   (ICIX) Intermedia Comm Fla I   04/29/98

Intermedia Comm Fla I-Daily 04/29/98 C=70.375 +5.375 O=63.750 H=70.875 L=61.750 V=2607500

"Obvious" Downtrend

Expansion Breakdown

*Abrupt Reversal

Additional Followthrough

REPRINTED WITH PERMISSION OF Omega Reserach Inc.
Chart created using SuperCharts 4.0.

Using Protective and Trailing Stops

Obvious trends attract the masses to one side of a market. As long as the trend stays intact additional players will continue to enter the market. At these junctures, it's easy to become complacent as the trend continues in your favor. However, you should "remain on your toes versus your heels" because you never know when it may end abruptly. These abrupt trend changes are caused when the masses (caught on the wrong side of the market) "run for the door" at the same time. Therefore, remaining nimble and using protective stops (initially) and trailing stops (should the market continue to move in your favor) is crucial. ICIX provides a good example. The stock has been in an obvious downtrend for the past few weeks. Yesterday, we had an Expansion Breakdown sell signal. Today, the stock opened at 63 3/4 and we go short. Soon after, the stock sells off 2 points. At this juncture, it's tough to play defense when you're feeling good about the position, but this exactly what you should do: a trailing stop should have been moved down to lock in at least 1/2 of the profits. The stock then reverses* and gains over 8 points from the lows. These abrupt turnarounds are usually caused when shorts, attracted by the obvious down trend, scramble to cover. When a trend is extremely obvious, you have to realize that there are many players already in the market. Therefore, instead of becoming complacent with the trend it is crucial to continue to use protective and trailing stops. Trading is never a game for resting on your laurels.

*Remember, gapping below the prior day's low and then trading back up through that low is another sign of a potential reversal (this is known as an "OOPS" pattern which was created by Larry Williams). Often these reversals can be a sign that the prior day's expansion in the direction of the trend may have been a climatic wash out, at least in the short run.

COOPER TRADING INC.
DAILY LEARNING SHEET
1 JUNE 1998

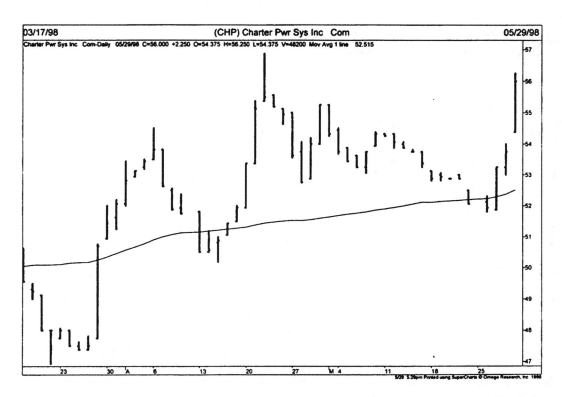

| 03/17/98 | (CHP) Charter Pwr Sys Inc Com | 05/29/98 |

Charter Pwr Sys Inc Com-Daily 05/29/98 C=56.000 +2.250 O=54.375 H=56.250 L=54.375 V=48200 Mov Avg 1 line 52.515

REPRINTED WITH PERMISSION OF OMEGA RESEARCH INC.
Chart created using Omega SuperCharts 4.0.

How To Anticipate Good Things Happening

On Wednesday night, I showed CHP as an Expansion Pivot buy. The stock closed well on Thursday and should be carried over. Today (Friday), CHP gapped open -- a sign of continued buying pressure -- and quickly ran up to 55 3/4 (up 2 3/8 points from our entry).

Many times after a signal, a stock will walk before it runs. As long as a position closes strongly in your favor after a strong impulse, it pays to hang on. I have often noticed stocks tend to have 3 day spurts before they pause again and contract. Remember the Hit And Run methodology is not just about intraday trading.

COOPER TRADING INC. DAILY LEARNING SHEET 2 JUNE 1998

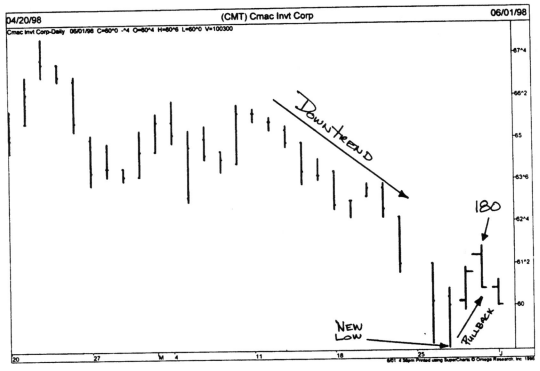

REPRINTED WITH PERMISSION OF OMEGA RESEARCH INC.
Chart created using Omega SuperCharts 4.0.

Holding Positions Overnight

I'm often asked when a position should be held overnight. In general, I prefer holding stocks that close well, those with size sellers (for shorts) near the close and those setups that are part of a pullback in a major trend. CMT (shown as a 180 short sale for Monday) meets all the criteria: it closes at its low, it has size sellers near the close and its setup was a pullback from new lows. The combination of these factors suggests that CMT has the potential to challenge those lows (around 59). Therefore, at least a piece should have been held overnight.

COOPER TRADING INC. DAILY LEARNING SHEET 4 JUNE 1998

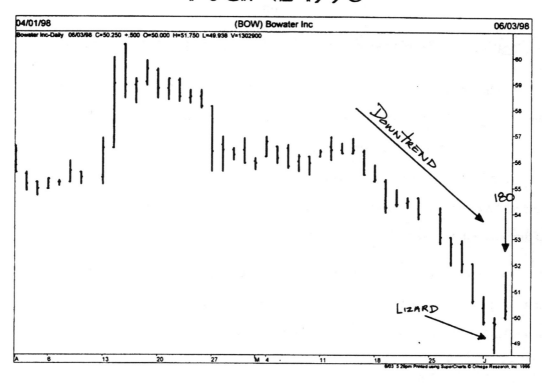

04/01/98   (BOW) Bowater Inc   06/03/98

Bowater Inc-Daily 06/03/98 C=50.250 +.500 O=50.000 H=51.750 L=49.938 V=1302900

If It's Not Going Up Then It's Going Down

In general, we trade with the trend and occasionally take a reversal pattern (i.e. Lizards and Gilligans) for the potential of a quick profit. If there is no follow-through, we should then once again look to trade in the direction of the underlying trend. BOW provides an interesting example of this concept. After a strong downtrend, BOW sells off and recovers to form a Lizard buy for Tuesday. This suggested that the downtrend was over (at least temporarily). Then, today, it rallies up nearly two points intra-day confirming a potential bottom. However, it fails and comes right back down to close near its low. This creates a 180 sell set-up for Thursday. The failed rally and pivot back into the direction of the underlying trend suggests that BOW's downtrend will continue. Remember: "If it's not going up then it's going down."

COOPER TRADING INC.
DAILY LEARNING SHEET
22 June 1998

[No Chart]

You've Got To Know When To Hold' em, Know When To Fold' em

Short-term trading is a game of hitting singles. A consistent contact hitter scores often and stays in the game while those whose constantly swing for the fences, strike out the most and may not be around to play the "next season." That being said, it is vital to let a winning position run for a few days. The occasional big winner will more than make up for many scratches. I've mentioned before the tendency for stocks to have 3 day spurts of momentum and the notion that stocks often walk before they run (it trickles before it pours)!

Let's take a look back at two Small Cap recommendations on the fax dated June 17. VOD triggered on Wednesday (the 17th) at 115 7/8, closing strongly each day and trading to as high as 121 11/16 on Friday. PLT triggered on Wednesday at 45 3/8 and traded to as high as 49 1/8 on Friday.

The Hit And Run methodology is not just about day trading. Allowing a stock to run for a few days while utilizing trailing stops will enhance your performance.

COOPER TRADING INC.
DAILY LEARNING SHEET
WEDNESDAY, 2 SEPTEMBER 1998

Beckman Instrument In-Daily 09/01/98 C=50.000 -5.375 O=52.500 H=52.750 L=49.938

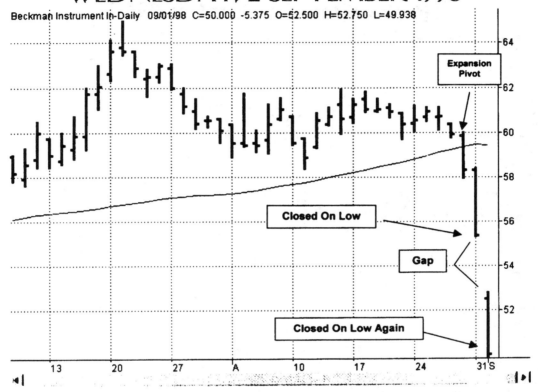

REPRINTED WITH PERMISSION OF OMEGA RESEARCH INC.
Chart created using Omega SuperCharts 4.0.

Surprises Happen In The Direction Of The Trend/Carrying Positions Overnight

In this week's Market Monitor, I mentioned that surprises happen in the direction of the trend. BEC's action during that 500 point "surprise" and today's bounce provides a good example of holding overnight and how the surprise theory applies to individual stocks. After hitting all-time highs, BEC begins to sell off. Then on Friday, it forms an Expansion Pivot for Monday. We go short and the stock closes at its low. This is a sign that at least a piece should be held overnight. Then today, in spite of a strong market opening, the stock gaps down nearly 3 points. Furthermore, in spite of a massive rally, the stock cannot snap back and closes on its low for the second consecutive day. This bearish action suggests that at least a piece should have been carried over once again. As you can see, surprises tend to happen in the direction of the trend. Also, when a stock bucks the overall market, it may be talking. Keep these things in mind when deciding whether or not to carry a position overnight.

COOPER TRADING INC.
DAILY LEARNING SHEET
Wednesday, 21 October 1998

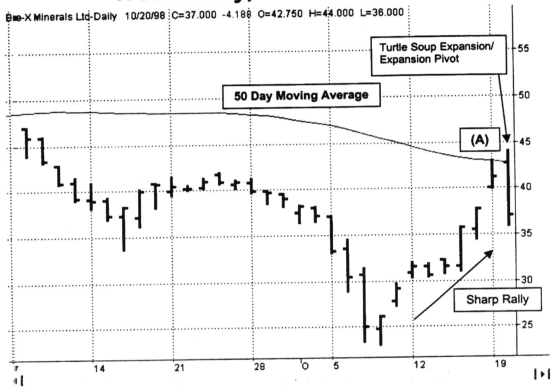

Bre-X Minerals Ltd-Daily 10/20/98 C=37.000 -4.188 O=42.750 H=44.000 L=36.000

REPRINTED WITH PERMISSION OF OMEGA RESEARCH INC.
Chart created using Omega SuperCharts 4.0.

Multiple Signal Failure At The Fifty

In Hit and Run Trading, I discussed that the 50 day moving average is significant because institutions and traders use it as a benchmark indicator. When a stock fails at the fifty it may be talking. Let's look at the recent action in BXM. After a sharp rally with virtually no pullbacks, the stock stops right at the 50 day moving average (A). Then today, it gaps above the average and attempts to rally. However, it caves in to form a multiple Turtle Soup Expansion/Expansion Pivot sell set-up for Wednesday. This was caused as the "Johnny come lately's" rush into the stock and are immediately trapped on the wrong side of the market. This multiple signal failure at the fifty suggests that the rally from lows may be over.

COOPER TRADING INC.
DAILY LEARNING SHEET
Friday, 23 October 1998

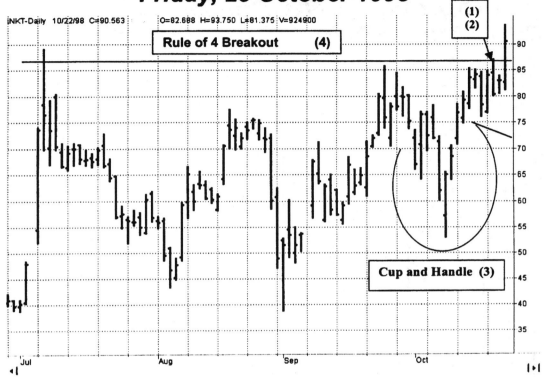

INKT-Daily 10/22/98 C=90.563   O=82.688 H=93.750 L=81.375 V=924900

Rule of 4 Breakout   (4)

(1)
(2)

Cup and Handle (3)

Jul   Aug   Sep   Oct

REPRINTED WITH PERMISSION OF OMEGA RESEARCH INC.
Chart created using Omega SuperCharts 4.0.

Anticipating Breakouts With Signals At/Near Multiple Tops: INKT

Legendary trader Bernard Baruch described successful trading as "anticipating the anticipators." How true. As you've heard me say before—many times breakouts are followed by 1 to 2 days of slight pullback. (1) I've also talked about the notion that powerful trends are seldom derailed by first or second sell signals. Rather these are usually quick flush outs. (2) I've also mentioned many times the benefit of looking at the short-term Hit and Run signals in the context of somewhat bigger picture patterns. Using these kinds of pieces helps me in selecting set-ups for us. I'm always asked how I differentiate between the many signals to focus on a few (and focussing on a handful of set-ups is the key to participating in a move—you just can't be all over the board and expect to maximize your trading potential). Let's take a look at INKT and you'll see why I chose the set-up for Thursday's sheet and why I focussed on the stock this morning, the breakout of 10/20 reversed leaving INKT with a Gilligan (1) (2). However, the stock never followed through to the downside (when signals don't trigger, the stock is often talking) instead, staying "inside" in a relatively narrow range day.

Now let's look at the bigger picture: the stock has a cup and handle formation (3) at triple tops! You've heard me refer to the power of rule of 4 breakouts (breakouts over triple tops) before: INKT's action on Thursday is testimony to the explosive potential of these kinds of breakouts. You might think of them as Flat Top Expansion Breakouts on a weekly chart. Lastly, why did I concentrate on INKT this morning? — in spite of a Dow down as much as 90 points, the tech-laden NASDAQ remained firm – a plus. Moreover, INKT is a great example of the (intra day) relative strength trading strategy. Take a look at intra day charts of INKT versus the S&P Futures. INKT refused to go down when the futures pulled back. Instead, the stock made higher highs. Finally, when the futures broke out in the last hour and a half, INKT exploded. The relative strength of the stock against the futures throughout the session was the tip-off. Learn to listen to stocks talk to you. Their behavior is telling. I hope you all participated in the move.

COOPER TRADING INC.
DAILY LEARNING SHEET
Monday, 23 November 1998

BCST-Daily 11/20/98 C=64.125 +7.000 O=59.250 H=64.750 L=58.000

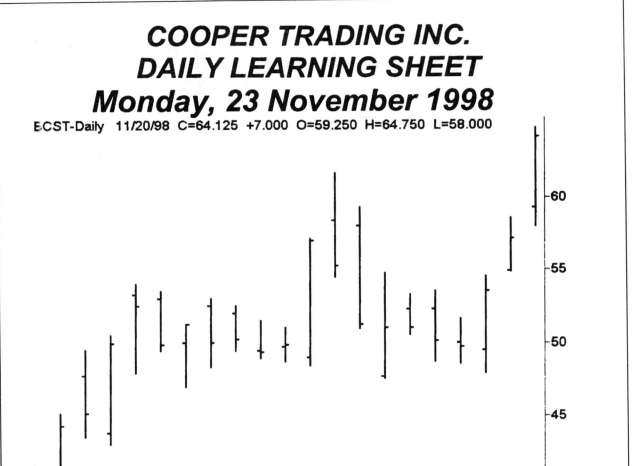

REPRINTED WITH PERMISSION OF OMEGA RESEARCH INC.
Chart created using Omega SuperCharts 4.0.

Staying With Winners

On the fax dated 11/19 (for Thursday) I showed a V-Thrust buy set-up on BCST. The signal triggered at 54 7/8 with a strong high to close ratio (in the top quadrant of the days range). Friday the stock gapped open again and after some sight bleed back into the prior days range, ran up an additional 7 points. When a stock closes strongly in your favor it's a good idea to carry over the position. This is particularly true if the stock is just coming off a pull back (as was the case with BCST). The <u>outside day</u> V-Thrust, and the gap up the next day without any bleed back were clues to a momentum move and further gains. Stocks with very little bleed back into the prior days range are often a positive sign of substantial buying pressure.

COOPER TRADING INC.
DAILY LEARNING SHEET
Friday, 04 December 1998

JBL-Daily   12/03/98 C=62.000 +1.562 O=60.375 H=65.125 L=60.063

REPRINTED WITH PERMISSION OF OMEGA RESEARCH INC.
Chart created using Omega SuperCharts 4.0.

Staying With Winners And Capturing Profits With Trailing Stops

The cornerstone of the Hit and Run Method is minimizing losses and maximizing gains. Both of these goals are accomplished thru the use of protective stops and trailing stops. Let's look at JBL which was a multiple buy set-up on the fax dated 12/02 (Wednesday). After triggering us long at 59 3/4, JBL closed near its high (60 7/16) and importantly also closed at a new closing high. Thursday, JBL opened flat and trended up cleanly to 65 1/8. A trailing stop placed in the 63 7/8 to 64 area preserved a solid gain as the stock sold off to 62 in sympathy with the markets last hour drubbing.

COOPER TRADING INC.
DAILY LEARNING SHEET
Tuesday, 22 December 1998

Bre-X Minerals Ltd-Daily   12/21/98 C=57.750 +2.125 O=55.125 H=61.000 L=55.125

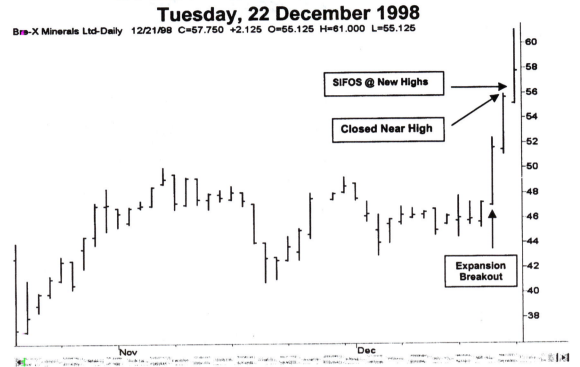

REPRINTED WITH PERMISSION OF OMEGA RESEARCH INC.
Chart created using Omega SuperCharts 4.0.

Managing Positions

Short term trading is a game of inches and feet and only occasionally yards. Therefore, it's important for us to manage the big winners properly through carrying overnight, adding to the positions and trailing stops. Let's look at BXM. Last Friday, I showed it as an Expansion Breakout. The stock rallied nicely and closed near its high. This is a sign that it should be held overnight. Then this morning, there is a size bid at 09:49 for 5,000 shares at 55 ¾. This is a good time to add to your position as the bid is near the new high (Stepping In Front Of Size At New Highs). The stock then takes off and trades over 5 points higher. With such large profits, this is a good time to begin to lighten up or at the least trail your stops. The stock gives back some of its gains and begins to trade sideways for the next 4 hours. At this juncture, you should continue to tighten your stops as the move may be over. Finally, in the last hour of trading the stock begins to sell off and gives up half of the day's gains. By now your stops should have been tight enough so that decent gains were captured on any remaining shares in spite of the sell off.

Because large gains are often few and far between, it's important for us to manage positions properly through carrying overnight when a stock closes well, using SIFOS to add to positions and trailing stops to protect profits.

COOPER TRADING INC.
DAILY LEARNING SHEET
Friday, 07 May 1999

PMCS Intraday

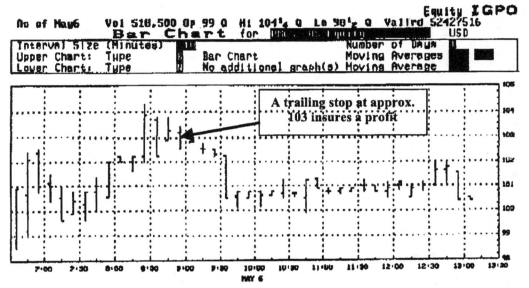

PPRINTED WITH PERMISSION OF BLOOMBER LP.

The Importance of Using Trailing Stops

Thursday's action demonstrates why the cornerstone of successful short-term trading is founded on the use of trailing stops. Set-ups are simply that--- set-ups. There is no guarantee that the best set-up, with multiple signals, size to buy, bells and whistles, what ever will lead to profits. Trading is an art more than a science. No methodology, no black box will print money, but you can capture profits by being a hands-on trader employing trailing stops.

Last night's sheets had a few set-ups trigger creating solid profits only to see the stocks fade. PMCS showed nearly a 5 point gain from entry before sliding back. On the big cap sheet, RAZF ran up over 5 points before collapsing. ABOV (also on the big cap) ran up 4 points as well before reversing.

Don't be afraid to ring the cash register because you hope the stock will come back or because you missed the high tick. The object of the game is to make money, not to pick tops and bottoms!

Using trailing stops is the key to unlocking the Hit and Run methodology.

CLOSING THOUGHTS

●●

I've often been asked what is the most important character trait of a winning trader. In my opinion it is having the ability to combine trading science with trading art. The science is the mechanical rule "buy 1/16 above yesterday's high" that anybody can follow. The art is the harder part. It's the ability to "sniff out things" and the ability to constantly ask yourself what's going on. As you can see from the previous pages, I am always putting pieces together and asking myself what is happening now, why is it happening, and how can I take advantage of it.

Can you be successful simply trading my setups on a mechanical basis? Maybe. But you will become much more successful when you learn to combine the tangible factors (the science) with the intangible factors (the art). This is what I hope you have learned from these lessons.

Best of luck in your trading,

Jeff Cooper

HIT AND RUN DAILY TRADING SERVICE
—FOR DAY TRADERS!

"Jeff's come up with a winning methodology. And if you think about it, it has to work. He only takes a position if momentum reasserts itself and, while the maximum loss he incurs is one point, the maximum profit is unlimited. Stack those odds in your favor and you should get exactly what I found; more wins than losses and the average win being greater than the average loss."

Gary Smith
TheStreet.com

A daily fax from Jeff Cooper which identifies the best three- to five-stock buy and short-sale recommendations based on his Hit and Run strategies.

Two levels of services are available:

The first service is his **Small Cap Trading Service** (limited to 100 traders) which focuses on those stocks whose average daily volume is under 200,000 shares per day. As a member to this service, you will receive via fax:

- The best **Small Cap Hit and Run Setups** for the upcoming trading day. You will be able to focus on the stocks Jeff believes will provide you with the best opportunities each day.

- Jeff acts as your personal mentor in his **Learning Sheet** which arrives three times per week and teaches you how to become an even better trader.

- His **Hit List** which reflects the best trending stocks to trade each week.

- The **Weekly Market Monitor** sent to you each Sunday night with Jeff's comments for the upcoming trading week.

- A free subscription to the **Big Cap Service**.

- A copy of Jeff's new audio tape *Trading the Stock Market for a Living*.

The cost of the **Small Cap Trading Service** is:

$1,920 for 6 months • $1,080 for 3 months • $400 for I month

The second service is Jeff's **Big Cap Trading Service** and is open to all traders. As a member, you will receive via fax:

- The best daily **Big Cap Trading Setups** from the stocks whose average daily volume is greater than 200,000 shares per day.

- His **Hit List** for the best trending Big Cap stocks to focus on daily.

- The **Weekly Market Monitor** with the outlook for the upcoming week.

The price of the Big Cap Trading Service is:

$600 for 6 months* • $375 for 3 months • $I50 for I month

*Also includes Jeff's audio tape Trading the Stock Market for a Living.

Also, upon subscribing to either service, you will be sent free Jeff's 10-page *Trading Tactics* booklet. This booklet will teach you specific trading strategies and money management strategies to help you maximize your trading effectiveness.

TO ORDER CALL: 1-800-797-2584 or 1-213-955-5777 (outside the U.S.)
OR FAX YOUR ORDER TO: 1-213-955-4242
OR MAIL YOUR ORDER TO: M. Gordon Publishing Group, 611 W. Sixth Street, Suite 2870, Los Angeles, CA 90017
www.mgordonpub.com
All orders please add $6 + $1 each add'l item; Priority Mail: $8 + $1 each add'l item; Airborne Int'l: $25 for shipping and handling.
California residents include 8.25% sales tax.

Other Books from M. GORDON PUBLISHING GROUP

THE 5 DAY MOMENTUM METHOD

JEFF COOPER

61 Pages   Spiral Bound $50.00

Strongly trending stocks always pause before they resume their move. *The 5 Day Momentum Method* identifies three- to seven-day explosive moves on strongly trending momentum stocks. Highly recommended for traders who are looking for larger than normal short-term gains and who do not want to sit in front of the screen during the day. *The 5 Day Momentum Method* works as well shorting declining stocks as it does buying rising stocks. Also, there is a special section written for option traders.

STREET SMARTS
High Probability Short-Term Trading Strategies

LAURENCE A. CONNORS
AND LINDA BRADFORD RASCHKE

245 Pages   Hard Cover $175.00

★ ★ ★ ★ (out of 4 stars) . . . Excellent!
Commodity Traders Consumer Report

Published in 1996 and written by Larry Connors and New Market Wizard Linda Raschke, this 245-page manual is considered by many to be one of the best books written on trading futures. Twenty-five years of combined trading experience is divulged as you will learn 20 of their best strategies. Among the methods you will be taught are:

- **Swing Trading**—The backbone of Linda's success. Not only will you learn exactly how to swing trade, you will also learn specific advanced techniques never before made public.

- **News**—Among the strategies revealed is an intraday news strategy they use to exploit the herd when the 8:30 A.M. economic reports are released. This strategy will be especially appreciated by bond traders and currency traders.

- **Pattern Recognition**—You will learn some of the best short-term setup patterns available. Larry and Linda will also teach you how they combine these patterns with other strategies to identify explosive moves.

- **ADX**—In our opinion, ADX is one of the most powerful and misunderstood indicators available to traders. Now, for the first time, they reveal a handful of short-term trading strategies they use in conjunction with this terrific indicator.

- **Volatility**—You will learn how to identify markets that are about to explode and how to trade these exciting situations.

- Also, included are chapters on trading the smart money index, trading Crabel, trading gap reversals, a special chapter on professional money management, and many other trading strategies!

THE BEST OF THE PROFESSIONAL TRADERS JOURNAL SERIES

FROM LARRY CONNORS

Market Timing
42 Pages   Soft Cover $39.95

Learn how to determine which way the Dow, S&Ps, and Nasdaq are going the next day. Professional traders often use sophisticated tools and indicators to help them determine market bias for the next day. Larry Connors gives you his best strategies for determining market direction for the next day in an easy-to-understand and easy-to-use format. Learn how Larry exploits the VIX and TRIN indicators to successfully trade the markets. Backtesting results on just one of the strategies contained in this book has yielded a 288 percent return in just four years!

Includes the Connors VIX Reversal I–V, TRIN Reversals, TRIN Thrusts, and Percent Advance/ Decline Indicator (PADI).

Options Trading and Volatility Trading
55 Pages   Soft Cover $39.95

Ninety-seven percent of options traders lose money. Professional trader Larry Connors shares his best options trading strategies with you to help you avoid being just another losing trader. By exploiting stock splits and pricing inefficiencies as well as applying his own strategy, the Connors VIX Reversal, Larry delivers four powerful options methodologies that move the odds decidedly in your favor. In addition, Larry also provides you with the latest research on the little-known, but powerful indicator, historical volatility. From concept to action, Larry explains to you step-by-step how to best use historical volatility to conquer the futures, stock, and options markets.

Includes Trading Volatility with Options, Trading Options with the Connors VIX Reversal, Options on Stock Splits, and Exploiting Over-Priced Stock Sector Options.

Day Trading
44 Pages   Soft Cover $39.95

Everyone who wants to trade professionally must have this book. In it, Larry Connors shares five strategies that will help you become a top-notch day trader. These strategies represent the culmination of over 15 years of trading experience. Larry shows you how to use the powerful ADX indicator to become a winner in the stock market and in the S&Ps. Jeff Cooper also contributes his time-proven Torpedoes strategy to exploit the stock market on an intraday basis. Find out how real traders read the markets during the day.

Includes the 15-Minute ADX Breakout Method, Trading the 15-Minute ADX Breakout Method with Equities, S&P Momentum Day Trading System, Front Running the S&P's, and Torpedoes.

Best Trading Patterns, Volume I
41 Pages   Soft Cover $39.95

Trading is a war and only those traders who are properly prepared will succeed in battle. In *Best Trading Patterns, Volume I*, Larry Connors provides you with an arsenal of short-term trading patterns to successfully trade both stocks and futures. Larry takes you step-by-step through each strategy in this book and defines for you exact entry and protective stop points. If you trade based on gaps, volume, or pullbacks, this book contains the strategies that teach you to successfully trade them all!

Includes The Crash, Burn, and Profit Trading Strategy, Double-Volume Market Top Method, Bottom Reversals, Large-Range Days, Momentum Gaps, Triple-Day Pullbacks, and Turtle Thrusts.

Best Trading Patterns, Volume II
58 Pages   Soft Cover $39.95

If you can't get enough of Larry Connors' time-tested, market-proven, short-term (three- to seven-day holding periods) trading strategies, this is the book for you. Successful trader and hedge fund manager Larry Connors gives you seven potent technical trading strategies to conquer the stock and futures markets. Unlike other trading books that talk *around* trading, Connors' *Best Trading Patterns, Volume II* gives you exact rules for entry along with several illustrated examples to show you how these strategies have traded in the past. This book is designed to get you from reading to trading immediately.

Includes the Spent Market Trading Pattern, 1-2-3-4s, The 8-Day High/Low Reversal Method, 10% Oops, Momentum Moving Averages, Gipsons, and Wide-Range Exhaustion Gap Reversals.

HIT AND RUN TRADING
The Short-Term Stock Traders' Bible
JEFF COOPER
160 Pages   Hard Cover $100.00

Written by professional equities trader Jeff Cooper, this best-selling manual teaches traders how to day-trade and short-term trade stocks. Jeff's strategies identify daily the ideal stocks to trade and point out the exact entry and protective exit point. Most trades risk 1 point or less and last from a few hours to a few days.

Among the strategies taught are:

- **Stepping In Front Of Size**—You will be taught how to identify when a large institution is desperately attempting to buy or sell a large block of stock. You will then be taught how to step in front of this institution before the stock explodes or implodes. This strategy many times leads to gains from 1/4 point to 4 points within minutes.

- **1-2-3-4s**—Rapidly moving stocks tend to pause for a few days before they explode again. You will be taught the three-day setup that consistently triggers solid gains within days.

- **Expansion Breakouts**—Most breakouts are false! You will learn the one breakout pattern that consistently leads to further gains. This pattern alone is worth the price of the manual.

- Also, you will learn how to trade market explosions (Boomers), how to trade secondary offerings, how to trade Slingshots, and you will learn a number of other profitable strategies that will make you a stronger trader.

HIT AND RUN TRADING II
Capturing Explosive Short-Term Moves in Stocks
JEFF COOPER
212 Pages   Hard Cover $100.00

212 fact-filled pages of new trading strategies from Jeff Cooper. You will learn the best momentum continuation and reversal strategies to trade. You will also be taught the best day-trading strategies that have allowed Jeff to make his living trading for the past decade. Also included is a special five-chapter bonus section entitled, "Techniques of a Professional Trader" where Jeff teaches you the most important aspects of trading, including money management, stop placement, daily preparation, and profit-taking strategies.

If you aspire to become a full-time professional trader, this is the book for you.

SOFTWARE

FOR HIT AND RUN TRADING I

Omega TradeStation and SuperCharts Owners

Systems, indicators, and paintbars programmed by Stuart Okorofsky from the *Hit and Run Trading* manual by Jeff Cooper. Take five minutes to install these indicators into your TradeStation or SuperCharts library and you are ready to conduct nightly analysis on your database of stocks. This add-on module contains the complete set of indicators and systems for the *Hit and Run Trading* library. It also allows you to create a nightly report of setups that have been triggered from your database of stocks, and look at historical setups that have triggered for a particular stock. Compatible with versions 2.1 and higher of both TradeStation and SuperCharts.

Price—$175

Equis MetaStock Version 6.5 and Professional Owners

We have created a MetaStock add-on module for the Hit and Run Trading methodology. It contains Explorers and Expert Advisors. The Explorer is used to scan portfolios (limited only by the number of stocks in your database) for potential setups. The Expert Advisor will highlight and label potential setups.

Price—$175

FOR HIT AND RUN TRADING II

Omega TradeStation and SuperCharts Owners

We have created an add-on module for TradeStation and SuperCharts. The software identifies the patterns of *Hit and Run Trading II*. It alerts you to daily signals, plots entry and initial stop placement points, and allows you to scan a portfolio for setups. It also includes modules that will help you create the daily Hit List and identify potential candidates for Stepping In Front Of Size on New Highs and Lows™. The above is implemented using TradeStation and SuperChart's indicator and ChartScanner features.

The software comes with a complete user's manual to help you fully utilize the methods.

Price—$175

Equis MetaStock Version 6.5 and Professional Owners

We have also created an add-on module for MetaStock 6.5 and Professional. The software identifies the patterns of *Hit and Run Trading II*. It will scan a portfolio for daily signals and label the bars of the setups. It also includes modules that will help you create the daily Hit List and identify potential stocks for Stepping In Front Of Size on New Highs and Lows™. The above is implemented using MetaStock's Expert Advisor and Explorer features.

The software comes with a complete user's manual to help you fully utilize the methods.

Price— $175

There's Only One Place in the World You Can Find Trading Information Like This Every Day!

- Live teaching forums with some of the best traders in the world
- Daily access to proprietary indicators and strategies
- Interactive Relative Strength searches on over 5,000 stocks
- Intraday updates and commentaries

- Continuous, how-to articles on trading authored by professionals
- Quotes, live charts, news, research
- ... and much, much more!!!

WWW.TRADEHARD.COM
The Ultimate Super-Site for Traders
GO THERE NOW!

ABOUT THE AUTHOR

J eff Cooper is a full-time, professional equities trader. A graduate of New York University, he is also the author of *The 5 Day Momentum Method* and *Hit and Run Trading I* and *II*. You can read what Jeff has to say about the market daily at 11:30 A.M. EST at WWW.TRADEHARD.COM.